Following That Dream

From Elvis to Hollywood

Al Fleming

Published 2015.
Printed in the United States of America.

ISBN 978-1-937862-90-9
Library of Congress Control Number 2015935026

This book was published by BookCrafters,
Parker, Colorado.
bookcrafters@comcast.net

This book may be ordered from
www.bookcrafters.net
and other online bookstores.

Dedication

I dedicate this book to my Mother whose career kept her busy and allowed me to raise myself and go down the path in life I was destined to follow. She let me become the person I am today. And to my Father with his endless parade of characters, horse traders, outlaws and wheeler-dealers who gave me the lust for adventure, taught me the art of the deal and the love of history,

GOD BLESS THEM ALL!

"I really enjoyed Al's anecdotes in this book. Reading these funny moments put a big smile on my face!"

— Peter Brown

Table of Contents

Introduction..1
The Beginning...3
Elvis...7
Hollywood...18
The Beverly Hillbillies..18
Hollywood Fast Gun...20
A Wonderful Place...23
Oh Shit! The Casting Couch...26
A Step in Another Direction..31
Sam Peckinpah..37
The Getaway...50
Funny Happening...62
Burnt Offerings...64
The Lost Man..79
A Make-up Artist's Revenge...83
Winchester 73..88
Winterhawk...90
Oh Shit! Not This Old Boy..103
Nobdy Likes Flapping Eagle..106
The Las Vegas Show..110
How the West Was Won...115
Where Angels Go Trouble Follows...119
Slaughterhouse Rock...122
They Called Him Slim...125
Nakia...135
Anna and the King..138
Star Trek...141
Wild Bill..145

The Cherokee Kid..150
Adventures with Sam..154
Other Funny Tidbits...161
Roy Rogers..161
Hollywood Tough Guy...163
Hero...164
Tiptoeing Through the Tulips with Tiny Tim............168
Remembering...170
Revenge of a Soundman...172
Thinking Back..173
Planet of the Apes..174
A Funny Thing Happened in Hollywood...................175
The Legend of O.K. Freddie.....................................177
The Good Old Days...178
Becoming a Hollywood Make-up Artist.....................181
Adventures in Mexico...183
Corriganville..188
A Class Act Moses Comes to the Mountain................190
Funny Happening...194
A Wonderful Adventure..196

INTRODUCTION

Why does someone sit down and write a book? I have asked myself that question many times and have not come up with a definitive answer. I guess for my part it is the urging of friends to put my stories down in book form so others could enjoy them, also to preserve that little part of Hollywood history in which I was involved. Everyone wants to leave a little something behind when they are gone to say, "Hey I was here," and I am sure there is also a bit of ego involved.

In the last few years Hollywood and the world have lost some of the greatest personalities who ever graced the silver screen. Along with their passing goes some of the history of Hollywood that the average person will never know, some of the great stories, the insights and the fun of working in the Hollywood film industry. For years I have listened to many of the stories told while working with the stars and the character actors that are now gone, their stories never to be heard again for they were never recorded on paper or tape.

I hope some of the stories that I put down here will be of interest to someone, maybe even give you a good laugh or two. I have been very fortunate to have seen Hollywood in its glory days, to have met and worked with some of its greats and call some friends. The stories I relate here might seem crazy or unbelievable, but they are absolutely true and the way they happened. When reading them, remember Hollywood has nothing to do with the real world, it's not all sun glasses and autographs. It is populated by some of the world's most talented and crazy people.

I have been lucky to have been a part of it, and have loved every minute (almost). My life has been one adventure after another; I wouldn't have had it any other way!

Al Fleming

THE BEGINNING

I guess I should start by telling you something about myself, where I came from and how I ended up in Hollywood. So here goes!

I was born in the rural part of Florida's west coast in 1941. My Father raised and sold horses and anything else he could make a buck on. The first fifteen years of my life I worked on the ranch taking care of the stock and riding in the local rodeos. My mother and father decided to split company and I was sent to military school for a couple of years until I moved with my mother to a very small town called Homosassa Springs, Florida. At that time Florida was a paradise of unspoiled rivers, lakes and swamps.

I can't imagine growing up in a more beautiful place or at a better time. I spent most of my time exploring the rivers and swamps looking for Indian artifacts. I loved the solitude of the swamp, the adventure of seeing things that most white men had never seen. I would sometime spend days deep in the swamp with my trusty .22 rifle, a sack of peanut butter sandwiches and a head full of stories about the Seminole Indians and the legends that surrounded the swamp... Many times I would scare the shit out of myself remembering some of the legends, climb a tree and sit there for hours watching the dark parts of the swamp knowing there was something horrible out there just waiting to eat me ... it never did.

I think that most of the kids in my school thought I was stuck up or crazy for I was always a loner and a bit shy, I would rather be out in the swamp exploring than at most of the parties and doings in town. To this day I am still a bit of a loner and love to explore new things.

In high school I was on the football team, and the swimming and diving team, but didn't take them very seriously, but it was the only way to get girls in those days. In the small town of Crystal River, where I went to school, the football team was the most important thing happening so we players were treated like heroes. And hell, everybody wants to be a hero.

I quit school in the tenth grade (I wasn't learning anything anyway) and we moved to Guadalajara, Mexico for a little over a year. That year was one of the greatest learning experiences of my young life. I was in heaven with all of the history that was all around me. I got to explore parts of Mexico that most gringos never see. I loved the Mexican people and their colorful culture. While there I was involved in two gun battles, I fought bulls, taught congressmen how to fast draw and shoot a Colt single action pistol, but those are other stories.

In 1960 we moved back to Florida and the rivers I loved so much. To earn gas money I delivered moonshine whisky for our local sheriff who was an old hunting buddy and ran the largest moonshine stills in Citrus County. Later I started a little business called "The Paquet Boat," located at the Port Paradise Hotel and Lodge in Crystal River Florida. I taught skin diving and water skiing. I was lucky to own my own ski boat at that time, so was kind of self-employed. The business was somewhat successful; I made enough money to get by.

Then came the day in 1961 that changed my life. Early

one morning the life guard and pal of mine, Freddy Bunts, came into the shop and announced, "Elvis Presley is coming to town to make a movie, and he, and the cast and crew, would be staying here." At first I did not believe him, for Fred and I were always pulling pranks on each other and he knew I was an Elvis fan. Then after a few other people came in and told me the same thing, I started to think maybe it was true. If I ever had an idol that was not a cowboy, it was Elvis Presley. I had every record he ever made, even tried to grow sideburns and wore my hair long in a duck tail, I was a real fan.

As a kid growing up in the 1950s we had a small black and white television set that only got programming for about five hours a day. I was lucky to have pretty liberal parents that didn't put too many restrictions on me (heck I was a good kid). We would all gather around the TV at night to watch what was offered as programming in those days. One of the top shows then was the Ed Sullivan Show, which was a variety type show that showcased new and old talent. After Elvis appeared on the Ed Sullivan show the first time my dad would always remind me that crazy guy was going to be on the show that night. He would always sit there and watch Elvis and burst into laughter when he would do some of his gyrations, of course I would sit there in awe watching and loving every move Elvis made and when nobody was around would practice them myself.

As I said I was a real fan, and here I was about to meet my idol! The day came when the crew arrived; Hollywood had come to the swamp. I got to know some of them and their families, they seemed almost normal, to a country kid. One day a fellow came into the shop and asked about renting my ski boat and a couple of the scuba tanks. I told him what the daily rental rate was; he said that he would take it. When I asked him what day he wanted them he said until the end of the film. He introduced himself as Allen

Fortas, one of Elvis' buddies. I had just rented all of my equipment to Elvis Presley . . . shit this is great. *I am rich* I thought. Days passed slowly waiting for Elvis to arrive with his team, then it happened, the day that charged my life... THANK YOU ELVIS!

ELVIS

I will never forget the day that Elvis Presley, The King, arrived at Port Paradise resort and my life began to change. I hate to admit it but I was as excited as a young kid waiting for Santa Clause. On that day everything was a buzz, there were reporters from all the major television and newspapers and fans. I had never seen this many people in one place, everyone wanted to be the first to see Elvis. It was a real circus. I was one of them, I could not wait to see my idol, but had to stay close to the shop and take care of business. I heard screams from the fans and saw the crowd surge forward, I knew he had arrived. I saw absolutely nothing of his arrival, the crowd was too dense. I saw flash bulbs going off, girls and some old ladies screaming, police sirens blaring but nothing of the King. After a while some of the female staff came in and announced that Elvis was here!

It was crazy, something I had never seen before, people tried to surround his cabin, some even jumped into the water to get a better look, trying to get a glimpse of him. I spent most of the day running folks off my dock and out of my shop. After a while Allen Fortas came into the shop, big grin on his face. "What do you think of all this?" he asked.

"It's crazy man, those folks are nuts," I replied.

"Get used to it, it's always like this...Where is the local

lumber yard?" he asked. I gave him directions and he left. In an hour or so he returned with an arm load of freshly cut boards. I thought, *I bet they are going to board up the place or make clubs.* I found out later that the boards were for Elvis's karate practice.

The next morning as I opened the shop I saw Elvis and a couple of his buddies on the deck of his cabin which was directly across from my shop. Like a big dummy I just stood there and stared at him (hell, I had never seen a big star before), then we made eye contact and I didn't know what to do. I stood there with a dumb look on my face and my thumb in my ass. He grinned and said, "Hey man how you doing?"

As soon as my voice came back I replied, "Good."

When I went back into the shop I felt like a real dumb hick and felt I had made a fool of myself. I beat myself up for most of the day for not coming up with something cool to answer. That evening Alan came in and asked if I would take a few of the boys out and show them the river. As I gassed up the boat, Elvis came with two of his boys. He introduced himself (as if I didn't know who he was) shook hands and we were off. There I was on the river I loved so much with Elvis Presley...What could be better than that? I was in hog heaven, life was good. We talked a lot about different things and I found out he was just another country boy like me. I liked him right away, he was a really nice person and down to earth.

They began filming "Follow That Dream" the next day and I was invited to visit the set to watch them film. I was there before the sun came up not wanting to miss a thing. When the crew began to arrive and set things up, I was amazed at all the equipment it took to make a movie, I asked a lot of questions wanting to learn more about everything. It was a whole new world to me, one I would later learn to love.

A few hours later Elvis and his crew arrived and went to his dressing room, which was a very nice motor home. After a bit Alan came out to get coffee for the gang. He saw me standing there watching everything and he waived. "Good morning, glad you could make it. I'll be right back," he said. He took the coffee back to the motor home, stuck his head out the door and motioned me over. As I approached Elvis was standing in the doorway.

"Hey man come on in, hang out for a while." It was great to be just one of the guys, and I learned a few things. I never knew men wore make-up until I watched make-up man, Dan Striepeke, apply Elvis's make-up that first morning. I was really green and asked Allen if Elvis was a sissy. He laughed and told me that all actors wore make-up in films. Hell, I thought only sissies and women wore make-up, how was I to know that make-up was a big part of Hollywood film making?

Watching them film was a real treat for me. I never knew so much work went into making a movie or how many talented people were involved. As days went by I became friends with a couple of wonderful character actors, Harry Holcombe and Howard McNair, both great men that would help me a lot after I moved to Hollywood.

While hanging around the set one day, an assistant director came up to me and asked if I would like to make a quick fifty bucks. Of course I jumped at the chance, fifty bucks back in the 1960s was a nice little piece of change. I asked him what I had to do to earn that kind of money, and he told me that I had to double for and do a stunt for Elvis. I thought, *Oh Lord! What have I gotten myself into?* I had visions of something really dangerous that was most likely going to get me killed or at least cripple me.

He explained that all I had to do was jump out of the way of a car dressed in Elvis's clothes. After hearing that I got real brave, puffed my chest out and told him, "No problem I'm your man." We got the shot in one take. The whole crew applauded me for my great job, Elvis and the boys gave me the thumbs up. Right after that I had to go get larger size hats. Heck, I thought, *This Hollywood stuff is great, they pay you for something I would have done for free . . . I like it!*

One of my fondest memories of my time with Elvis happened about midway during the shooting of "Follow That Dream." My mother, bless her soul, was also an Elvis fan but would never admit it. Each day when I returned from the set, she would quiz me about what happened that day. I would tell her with much enthusiasm everything that I saw and about other goings on with the Hollywood bunch. After one of my many stories, which I always embellished a bit, she asked me if I thought Elvis and the gang might like a good home cooked meal for a change. Well the next day I told Allen that my Mother had invited them all to come over for a good old home cooked southern meal. Afterward I thought, *There is no way Elvis Presley would come to my little shack of a house and have dinner with my mother and me*, so I put it out of my mind. Later that evening as we were wrapping from the day's filming Elvis came over to me and asked, "Is your mom a good cook?"

"The best," I answered him.

A few days later Mother and I sat in our little house eating fried chicken and blue gills (a Florida fish) with Elvis, Allen and Lamar. My mother was on cloud nine, loving every minute of it. She was also a very good cook and enjoyed all of the compliments about her cooking. After we had consumed a huge amount of chicken (those boys could really eat!), Elvis saw her old piano and asked her if she played. She told him that she could not read music but played by ear for some of the local church gatherings. For the next few minutes she and Elvis played and sang some of the old gospel songs she knew. Everyone seemed to have a great time, and we all shared some great laughs that evening. To the day she passed away, that was one of her fondest memories and one of mine, also.

One of the most embarrassing things I can remember happening during my time working with Elvis occurred on July 4th while still in Florida. I had been hired to play Uncle Sam for a lavish Fourth of July party hosted by a very wealthy man named Charlie Lenz, who lived in Homosassa Springs. Charlie was an interesting guy who had made his millions selling insurance for Lloyds of London who insured Ringling Brothers and other circuses and fairs around the country. He had built a beautiful compound on a large piece of land right on the river. He was always fascinated that I spent almost all of my free time in the swamps collecting Indian artifacts and had taken a liking to me He would always give me any extra work that he needed done around the place.

Knowing that I worked and hung out with the movie folks, he asked me to invite Elvis and the gang to his party, which I did. I will never forget that evening. I was dressed in a red, white and blue satin Uncle Sam costume that had been rented somewhere, complete with cotton ball beard, mustache and eyebrows. I had been hired to check invitations and direct traffic to the parking area. My big hat was about two sizes too big and kept slipping down around my ears. I looked pretty silly.

In the distance I saw a big black limousine approaching and knew it was Elvis and the boys. I wanted to dive behind a tree or bush or something, how could I be cool dressed like a clown standing at a gate directing traffic? As they pulled up and stopped I tried to be as cool as one could be in that situation. The driver's side window rolled down and there was Lamar Fink, Elvis's three hundred pound driver, looking at me trying to keep a straight face. I welcomed him and gave him directions to the parking area. The rear window rolled down and Elvis was grinning at me, also trying not laugh. "Cool outfit, see you inside," he said and rolled up the window. I could hear the laughter from inside the limo as they drove off.

There I was, a teenaged kid who wanted to be cool in front of my idol and I looked like something out of a bad minstrel show. I was sure that I had blown any resemblance to cool I might have had. The next day I was almost too embarrassed to show up on the set. I think Elvis saw my problem. He came over and thanked me for inviting them to the party and as I tried to make excuses for myself, he looked at me and said, "Hey a man's got to do what a man's got to do, you were taking care of business!" I guess I should not feel too bad, I made a whopping twenty-five dollars for making myself look like an ass!

As happens so often in Florida the weather changed and it rained almost every day which slowed production. Alan came into the shop one day and told me that they were returning to the studio to finish the film there. My heart sank, I was more than upset. I was downright depressed. I was having so much fun I hated to see it all come to an end, and heck, I was pals with Elvis!

That night when I went home my Mother knew

something was wrong. She asked, "What's the matter?" I told her what had happened, and as Mothers do, she tried to make it better... it didn't really help, but God bless her for trying.

The next day at work I watched all my newly made friends start packing up to return to Hollywood, it was a hard day for me. That evening Allen came in and asked me to stop by Elvis's cabin before I went home to say goodbye. That evening after locking up I went over and knocked on the door and was invited in. I guess I looked like a whipped dog, for Lamar, one of the Memphis boys, asked, "What's up man? You look like you're on a downer."

I told them that I hated to see them all leave, and how much I enjoyed working with them. Elvis looked at me very seriously and said, "Hey man, come work with us on this film." It hit me like a Sunday punch ...

"What do you mean come with you, what the hell would I do in Hollywood?"

He grinned, "You'll work with us, we'll have a ball. What do you say?" It took me about two seconds to say yes.

That night I told my Mother that I was going to Hollywood to work for Elvis. "Like hell," she said, "You're not going anywhere, especially to Hollywood." Well after many hours of pleading she realized that I was going with or without her permission and gave up.

I sold my Indian artifact collection (which I regret to this day) for two hundred dollars, packed my 1956 Mercury and was off to Hollywood and a new life. So I can honestly say that Elvis Presley changed my life.

Some of my fondest memories were of my mother and Elvis sitting at the piano playing and singing together after one of her southern fried chicken dinners...THOSE WERE THE GOOD OLD DAYS. I will relate only one more Elvis story here, one I still find amusing.

At the time Elvis came to Florida to film "Follow That

Dream," his Father Vernon had just remarried and was coming to the location for Elvis to get to know and spend some time with his new family. It was impossible for him to have any quiet private time with them because of all the fans that surrounded Port Paradise twenty-four hours a day. A plan was formulated (I don't remember by who) that might work and give him and his new family some private time together. It turned out to be a good one and worked well.

Here's what happened, the limousine pulled up in front of his cabin, Alan rushed me out wearing some of Elvis's clothes, we jumped into the limo and it sped off. It was crazy, as we sped down the narrow two lane road it looked like a parade, for every fan who had car was now following us down the road. After we left, Elvis and his family went out to a nice private dinner away from the throngs of fans that always seem to follow him. We drove around for about an hour leading our parade as far away from Elvis as we could. It was great fun.

I could tell you more Elvis stories but won't. I think everyone who ever met him has written tell-all books, some true, others just plain bull! All I will say about him is that in the time I worked with him, I found him to be an honest, thoughtful, generous, lonely, kind person who did more for people than we will ever know. My life was truly changed by him and I will always be grateful for the day he came into my life. I miss him dearly!

In those early days, being a young kid, the only camera I had was a little Kodak Brownie camera that my Mother had given me. I did bring it to the set with me one day to get some shots and as luck would have it, the damn thing had a light leak so almost all of my shots came out a bit fuzzy…but that's better than nothing!

Many years later when my mother was living in Las Vegas, she loved playing the slot machines and was frequently at the Las Vegas Hilton playing in the high rollers' section. One day she called me and told me that I would not believe who she had been playing with. Well not being a mind reader I ask her who it was. "It was Colonel Parker," she replied. "He is living here in Las Vegas and loves the slots as much as I do. We play together almost every day, and he would like to see you." A few weeks later I was at the Hilton playing the slots with my mother and the Colonel.

It was good to see Colonel Parker again after all these years. I had always gotten along with him and liked him. I know he has gotten a bad rap for years about taking advantage of Elvis, but I don't believe a word of it, I never saw anything but love and respect between them for the short time I was around. I think the Colonel's hard shell exterior scared some of the guy's working with Elvis, but under that shell lurked a pussy cat. I found him funny and likable if given a chance. For years I asked him why he did not write a book telling his side of the story to set things straight, he would always reply, "One of these days!" Well here is a scoop, I know he was working on a book with his new wife or girlfriend before his death, I hope she will finish it and get it out so we can all know the other side of the Elvis and Colonel Parker story.

The last time I saw the Colonel I got up the strength to ask him the big question, IS ELVIS REALLY DEAD? He looked at me for a beat, a little grin came across his face, then he just winked at me. He never did answer my question. I would like to believe that Elvis is still alive out there enjoying a quite normal life somewhere knowing that millions of his fans still love him and his music. In my heart he will always be with me, when I think of him my memories always go back to a warm summer night in 1961 watching him on the porch of the shack from "Follow that Dream," holding the beautiful Ann Helm in his arms singing "Angel" to her.

I was truly lucky to have been in the right place at the right time to meet and become friends with Elvis Presley. God was surely looking over my shoulder. I don't think a day goes by that I don't think or remember something about him. Still as an older man, I get tears in my eyes and a lump in my throat every time I watch one of his movies!

I feel I must add something here just to keep the story straight!

Recently I have been made aware of a few newspaper and magazine articles written about my short time with Elvis that I had never seen before. In retelling my story, the writers, or so called reporters who I have never spoken to, found it necessary to elaborate on the facts and make the story bigger than it was, so I want to set things straight!

Those articles state that I went on to become Elvis's stunt double and stand in, which is not true. I did one stunt for Elvis while shooting "Follow that Dream" which was the only stunt I ever did for him. I was never his stand-in, nor was I part of the Memphis Mafia, maybe the Florida Mafia if there ever was such a thing. I never spent night and day with him. I was lucky enough to spend some very special times with him which changed my life. As stated before I was just a flunky, I ran errands and hung out for a short time doing whatever was needed to be done.

That's it, just wanted to keep the facts honest, my story is simple I don't need anyone to make it bigger than it was!

That summer of 1961 was truly a magical time for me and it seems a lot of other folks as well. Each April there is an Elvis celebration held in Inverness, Florida called "When Elvis Came to Town." Through the hard work of people like Wendy Stillwell and John Grannan, the small town of Inverness hosts thousands of fans from around the world who come to share their love for Elvis and to see where he made what I think is one of his best films. It amazes me that there are now tours of location sites and historical plaques where we shot the film, there are even roads named after him.

If you are a true Elvis fan, the celebration of the making of "Follow that Dream" is a must for you. There are plays about the filming, guided tours of the locations and lots of shared memories of some people who worked on the production and got to know Elvis. I hear there is even a new book just released about the making of the film. I know Elvis would be proud to know that there are so many folks who still and will always love him!

GOD BLESS THE KING!

HOLLYWOOD

Upon arrival in Hollywood I was like a kid in a candy store, I could not wait for each day to come. Remember, I was a true country bumpkin, I had never been in big city, and I was on my own starting a new life.

My first day at work was at Goldwyn Studios (still working on "Follow that Dream"). Entering the studio that first day was magic. I had never seen anything like that in my life. There were people in all types of costumes busily moving between the sound stages, sets being transported, props being sorted, actors rehearsing lines as they headed towards the stages where they would work. It was a wonderful magical place to me...God I loved it, I was in heaven. I thought, *This is where I belong, this is right where I want to be.*

During the filming I got to know a lot of great people who would become lifetime friends and help me learn the ropes of the film industry.

THE BEVERLY HILLBILLIES

The first acting job I had in Hollywood was on the television series "The Beverly Hillbillies." It was a real miracle. My first agent, Linda Britton of the Britton Agency, sent me on an interview for a part in the show. In those days I thought when you were given a script you had the part; I was really green in the way of the business. I went to the old Raleigh Studios for my interview. When I arrived on the lot I got a bit lost trying to find the right offices and began to panic for I didn't want to be late. As luck would have it, I spotted Donna Douglas, one of the stars of the show, coming towards me. I approached her and asked directions to the offices telling her I had a part on the show. She was very friendly and offered to escort me to the offices and introduce me to everyone, which she did. I met everyone and thanked them for the job, I must have looked foolish now that I think back, but I was new to that show business thing.

The director told me to go across the street to the Desilu Studios, see a casting director named Ruth Burch who was casting the show, and tell her I was there for the part. I did as I was told and when I found her office I walked right in unannounced. I was met with a cold stare for a few seconds then a very unfriendly, "And what do you want?" I explained that I was sent over by the director to see her because I was playing the part in the show! "You are, are you?" she asked. At this point I knew I had screwed up in some way and started to panic a bit, "How long have you been in the business?" she asked coldly.

I didn't know how to respond so I told her the truth, "I've been in it about an hour now!" With that she broke into uncontrollable laughter, She looked up at me still trying to control herself, "At least you're honest, I guess we will see if you can act."

I went on to work on the show three times each time playing the same character. I also fell in love with Donna Douglas but don't anyone tell her!!

HOLLYWOOD FAST GUN

I have always had a fascination for history and firearms. While in Florida I saved my money and bought a Colt single action pistol and learned to use it well while still a teenager. I saved and bought my first fast draw holster from the man who invented them, Arvo Ojala. I became very good at fast draw! One of the first things I did when I arrived in Hollywood was to visit Arvo's shop and get to know him. He taught me a lot about the sport of fast draw and got me interested in competition. I worked for him in my spare time in trade for lessons and equipment. At that time the adult western was the rage in Hollywood. Every major studio had a western series running on national television everyone was working. They were good times.

I competed in many fast draw contests held around the country and won quite a few. I was offered a sponsorship by Alfonso's Holster and Gun shop who was one of the world's top makers of fast draw holsters. I accepted the deal I was offered and went on to win many championships. At the shop we made custom rigs for a lot of the western stars of that era. We would close the shop on Thursday nights and teach the art of fast draw and fancy gun handling to many of them.

CHAMPIONS KNOW . . . .
that Alfonso's holster is the best on the market for

WALK & DRAW

Fred Stieler
National Champion
chooses Alfonso's

Al Fleming

One day while I was at the shop a man I recognized came in. He introduced himself as John Derek. He wanted a special holster rig made for a new series he was getting ready to start called "Frontier Circus." We worked on some ideas and came up with a design that we thought would work. The next couple of days I worked along with Alfonso to build the prototype. When it was done, I called John and told him that it was ready and asked if he would like to stop by and take a look at it. He explained that he was very busy getting ready for the first day's shooting and wondered if I could stop by his house on the weekend with the rig. I told him that I would be glad to.

He gave me directions and we set up a time to get together that weekend. I arrived at the agreed time and proceeded to the back yard gate as he had instructed me to do. I knocked on the gate but got no response—John had told me to just come on in if no one opened the gate. I opened the gate and walked into the back yard carrying my gun cases and John's prototype gun belt. To my horror I almost fell over a beautiful woman who was lying naked on beach pad sunning herself. I didn't know what to do. I must have turned five shades of red. In a quivering squeaky voice I apologized for bursting in on her, I must have looked really pitiful for she smiled and pointed to a corner of the yard, "John's over there, he's expecting you, I'm Ursula."

I looked where she pointed. There stood John laughing hysterically enjoying my situation; he waved me over. It took him a bit to stop laughing, and he slapped me on the back. "I guess you

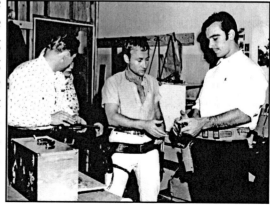

have met Ursula," he said. I apologized to him for bursting in on her. "No big deal. She's European. They're always naked over there; let's see the rig."

I handed him the prototype holster rig, he inspected it and seemed pleased. "Show me how it works." I strapped on the rig, broke out one of my pistols, holstered it and proceeded to show him how it worked, all in slow motion so he could see every move I made. After running through all the moves with him a few times, he asked me to show him how fast I could draw the gun with this new rig. I had practiced this draw for hours so that when I demonstrated it to him I would be very fast and smooth.

To show him this lightning fast draw I stepped back a few paces, got ready, then made the mistake of looking over at Ursula to see if she was watching …she was! The first attempt at my draw I dropped my gun and it nearly went into the pool. After retrieving it, I was a bundle of nerves, my heart was in my throat, I was a mess. John looked at me, "Nice draw!" he said with a laugh. "A bit nervous are you?"

After getting my voice back I explained that I was a nineteen year old young man with all my hormones running amok, and the fact that one of the most beautiful woman that I had ever seen in my life was lying naked just a few feet away, my concentration was zero. After a while I got my composure back and I was able to teach him how to use the new rig and he got very smooth and fast with it. We had many laughs about that day and it became a running joke with John. Every time he invited me over to his house he would assure me that Ursula had her clothes on.

John started filming his new series, "Frontier Circus," and he invited me to the set to visit and even got me a recurring cameo role of "Toby."

I found John to be a great guy with more talent than he was ever given credit for. Because he was very handsome, Hollywood cast him in a very narrow niche, never letting him prove himself with better roles. He proved himself later as a director/writer and a great still photographer.

A WONDERFUL PLACE

Hollywood was a great place to be during the 1960 and 70s. It was an era of hippies, free love and new forms of music that were changing the world. There were wonderful characters everywhere, each more outlandish than the other. And there were the girls everywhere, on the street corners, in the parks—they seemed to be come out of the woodwork. For a nineteen year old country boy it was paradise. I ate it up like a starved bear in a honey shop. I fell in love at least two times a week.

I discovered a place called Cafe Figaro which was owned by actor Bill Cosby, it was a wine and coffee type place catering to the artsy people and always had good entertainment in its lower rooms. The food was good and there were always some very talented people playing there. The first time I saw or heard of Cheech and Chong was in one of the small rooms in the basement of the club. I didn't know who they were or what to expect but heard that Janis Joplin was there, and I wanted to meet her so went down to see what was going on.

The small room was packed with hippies and a few celebrities and filled with smoke from marijuana cigarettes. Everyone was roaring with laughter and having a great time as I elbowed my way into the room. I saw Janis among a group of people across the room and made my way towards her inserting myself into the group. I just stood there not knowing what to say or how to introduce myself. The noise was too loud, and she was in no condition to have heard me or even know I was there. She was what you would call major fucked up—stoned out of her mind.

As I stood there I became aware of Cheech and Chong on the small stage and what they were doing. I started to get the act they were doing and realized that you had to be a "stoner or head" to really understand their comedy. Someone handed me a joint and said, "Hey man take a hit on this!" Well at that time, I did not have much experience in the smoking department but took a hit anyway. Oh my God in a few minutes I was one sorry puppy, it hit me like a ton of bricks. At first it scared me, but soon I got into it. I thought everything was funny and Cheech and Chong were killing me, I laughed so hard at what they were doing I could hardly keep standing.

Then the terrible munchies hit me. I was ready to chew the paint off the walls—I don't remember ever being that hungry. I figured my only chance to survive was to get upstairs and get some food, any food, but I must feed myself or someone was going to die. I stumbled out of the room but could not find the stairs, I was a mess. Luckily I was rescued by a pretty little hippie girl (at least I think she was pretty, but don't remember), we made it up the stairs and I remember eating lots of food but am not sure what it was. Everything from there on is a bit of a blur, I do remember waking up the next morning in an unfamiliar bedroom with a terrible headache and smelling like a goat. I got dressed quickly and made a hasty retreat without seeing anybody.

I guess I got hooked for after that evening the Cafe Figaro became my home away from home. My buddies and I always ended up there after work and stayed until it closed. We had some wonderful times there and saw and met some of the folks that change the face of music and comedy forever. I will tell you a funny story that happened to me one morning leaving the club.

A group of us had been partying pretty hard all night and were pretty messed up when the club closed at two in the morning. I stumbled to my car, got in and decided to have a couple hits on the pipe before starting home. As luck would have it, just as I took my last hit I saw a LAPD motorcycle cop pull in behind my parked car and hit his red light. *I am dead*, I thought. *My career is over. I'm about to be arrested for being drunk and high on marijuana.* My mind raced as I thought what to do. The only hope I had was to get out of the car quickly and meet him before he could smell the smoke inside my car. I quickly exited my smoke filled car and met him at the rear of my car. He looked at me, shinned his flashlight in my face, "What's wrong with your eyes?" he asked. "Have you been drinking?"

I was in a real panic, and blurted out, "I have been crying and have had a few drinks. When I got home from work today I found a note from my wife telling me that she was taking the kids and leaving me for another man,. So I have been crying a bit."

He came over patted me on the back and said, "Son, I know what you are going through I've been there myself. It'll all seem better in the morning, go home and get some sleep . . . Drive carefully!" He went back to his motorcycle and left. At times someone watches over fools and gives them a second chance, I was lucky that night. That is a true story!

OH SHIT THE CASTING COUCH!

After leaving Elvis I decided to try my hand at the acting profession and with a little help from my friends was signed with the Britton Agency, one of the leading talent agencies in Hollywood. Realizing that I was new to the business, they enrolled me in various acting classes to teach me acting skills. After a few months of classes I had head shots done (8x10 photos) and they sent me out on casting calls. The first few interviews I screwed up pretty badly; I had beginners' nerves. I was so nervous by the time I showed up for my readings, I could hardly remember my own name, much less pages of dialog. I thought about quitting but being a tenacious sort, I was determined to see it out.

As time passed and I grew more confident in my abilities as an actor, I was able to land a few small parts in television westerns such as "Wagon Train," "Lawman," "Laramie," "The Virginian," and a few others. I was pretty full of myself for everything seemed to be working, and the parts just kept on coming my way. Not only was I an actor, but I could do my own stunts and was training some of the stars of the various series how to handle a six-guns, which opened a lot of doors. In those days everything you could do helped get you work in Hollywood. I guess in today's Hollywood it would be called professional ass kissing!

One day Linda Britton, the head of the agency, called me into her office. I could see that she was excited as she sat me down. "I have good news," she told me. Warner Brothers wanted me to do a screen test for one of the lead rolls in a new western television series. They had liked my work in one of the early "Cheyenne" shows that I had done for them. Needless to say I was more than happy, this could be my big break, and it could make my career if I didn't blow it!

The next day I reported to the Warner Brothers casting offices to meet Solly Biano who was head casting agent there. We had a very cordial professional meeting, and everything seemed to be going well. He gave me the rundown about the new series and about the character I would play. I was given the script to take home and study and the screen test was scheduled for the next afternoon. As I left his office I was on cloud nine, I could already see myself doing the series and becoming one of Warner's new young western stars. When I reported for the screen test, I knew my lines forward and backward, I was ready for my big day. We shot the test and everything went perfectly, I got slaps on the back from some of the crew and even Solly seemed pleased. I went home that evening certain I would get a call the next day to sign me to the series but nothing happened.

A week later my agent called me in for another meeting. She told me that I was almost certain to get the series, that the people over at Warner's had watched the test and had liked what I had done, they wanted to meet with me again that afternoon to discuss the contract. Walking through the gates at Warner Brother studio that afternoon I was strutting my stuff, my ego was inflated to the bursting point, I thought to myself, *Kid, you have it made!* At a private meeting that day I met the director and producers of the new show and a few of the other casting people. The meeting went just fine and everyone seemed to like me. *I had it made*, I thought.

After everyone left Solly's office he began explaining

how the contract would work and the demands it put on me. Basically I had to enroll in the acting classes there at the studio, get new head shots made and meet some of the other big shots at the studio. Well this seemed to be a reasonable request being that I was pretty new to the business and I agreed to it. He told me that he would set up a few more meetings in the next few days and after meeting with everyone we would sign the contract to do the series. I had meetings with drama coaches, photographers, publicity people, wardrobe folks and make-up people. They set up photography sessions, taking stills in every type of costume you can imagine and many make-up changes, it was all a blur there for a while, but I loved every minute.

Then came the day that my agent called and told me they were ready to sign me to a contract to do the series. I can't even tell you how excited I was as I drove over the Warner's that day, I was like a kid waking up Christmas morning and finding a room overflowing with every toy ever wanted.

As I entered Solly's office that day he was all smiles and greeted me warmly, there was a stack of contracts along with some of the photographs we had taken there on his desk. "I guess your agent told you that we are ready to sign you to a three year contract today and there are certain stipulations that have to be met before signing." Everyone working there had gone through that process. He started laying out the stipulations: I must take private acting lessons which the studio would take care of. I must move into an apartment across from the studio to be closer to my work and do some personal appearances to promote the series and meet the gay boy set!

Well, being from the swamps of Florida and fairly new to the Hollywood scene I did not know what or who the gay boy set was. I asked him what the gay boy set was, he gave me an odd look and replied, "You know the gay boys." I really did not know what he was talking about and told him so. He looked at me like I was crazy, I guess he thought I was pulling his leg—guess I shouldn't say that, for he would have liked me to do just that. "The gay boy set, you know the gay boys!"

Then it hit me. "Do you mean the fairies, the queers?" I ask him.

"We don't call them that out here. They are called gay boys."

Being a bit dense and slow to catch on I continued, "Well what does that mean?"

"Get to know them, hang out with them, they can be a big help to you in this business."

Well I began to get his meaning and my anger started to build, this was not what I had expected or wanted to have anything to do with. As I tried to control my anger I thought maybe I was misunderstanding his meaning, maybe he didn't really mean what I thought he was telling me. "I don't understand exactly what you are asking me to agree to."

"All you need to do is to get to know a few of the fellow's, hang out with them, attend a few parties, be seen around town with them … I will teach you all you need to know. It's no big deal. It's part of the contract, everyone here at Warners does it!"

At this point my anger and disappointment got the best of me, I could control it no more, I began to tremble with anger and rage. I reached across his desk, grabbed him by the shirt and pulled him across his desk. I was ready to kill the little bastard but something stopped me. I dropped him and in a voice that I wanted to be booming and as macho as possible told him to fuck himself and stick the contract up his ass. Of course, the voice that came out was high pitched squeaky Mickey Mouse sounding, something that always happens when I get really angry.

I stormed out of his office that day, but I can still hear his shouts of "You'll never work in this business again. Your career is over!" At that point I was so mad and disappointed that the first thing I did was get to a phone and call my agent. I told her that if this was what one had to do to become an actor in that town that I wanted no part in it. That day I quit wanting to be an actor and started doing stunt work. The acting bug would not bite me again until a few years later.

A STEP IN ANOTHER DIRECTION

As a child I was always interested in art. My parents had me take the drawing test that, in those days, was in the back of almost every comic book. Draw a picture of Mickey Mouse, send it in and see if you had any talent. Of course everyone that drew the damn thing passed and by sending in thirty dollars you were enrolled in the Famous Artist School of Art. Of course it was a scam, and your artistic talents were not improved one bit.

As a kid my family was pretty poor and sometimes it was hard for my parents to make ends meet. We lived on a ranch and raised horses but had chickens, goats and the usual critters you expect to see so we always ate well. Most of my toys I made of clay and got pretty good at that. As someone once said if I hadn't been a boy, I wouldn't have had anything to play with! So there you have it, my great art experience! Moving ahead …

While working with Elvis I got interested in make-up by watching the make-up artist on "Follow That Dream" every morning. I ask him if he would do a make-up job on me for a costume party I was going to attend. He turned me into an old man, mustache and all. I was amazed, for when I went to the party nobody recognized me. I had a ball!

Jump ahead a few years, to when I was in Hollywood. I

just had my first casting couch experience and was not going down that road. I had quit my agent so my income was in the crapper. I worked at Corriganville Movie Ranch doing stunt shows and fast draw demonstrations on the weekends and made a whopping five dollars a day which was top dollar wages there. While working there I got a good stunt job on Rex Allen's Craft Music Hall television show doing a stagecoach chase, transfer and fight with Rex. It was a pretty easy job. All I had to do was chase the coach, do a transfer from my horse onto the running stage, climb up on top and fight with Rex's stunt double, and take a fall from the stage into Robin Hood Lake that was below a small cliff alongside the stage road. No big deal, right?

Well what I didn't know was that the stage driver had never driven a six-up team of horses and as I mounted the stage and began my fight he lost control of the team on the narrow road where we were filming so the timing of the stunt was off. As we rounded the curve where I was to take my fall from the stage, we were way off our mark, but I had no way of knowing that. As I began my fall I was thrown off balance, and as I fell, I caught the back wheel. It launched me over the cliff into the lake below. When I hit the water I was out cold, and if there hadn't been a safety man in the lake, this book would not be written.

When I woke up I was in the hospital with a body cast from my rear-end to my neck, the only thing touching the bed was my head. I had broken my back in two places. They told me that I would most likely never walk again because of nerve damage. Time passed and after nearly two months in the hospital I began to get some feeling back in my legs. My body cast was removed, but I was still in traction and they still told me not to get my hopes up. I am a stubborn cuss, so little by little I began forcing myself to do things they told me I should not do.

One day I shuffled myself into the bathroom without anyone knowing, got dressed and escaped from the hospital, got a cab and went home. I had a frantic call from the hospital when they discovered I was missing telling me that they would not be responsible for what might happen to me if I did not return at once. I explained that they had told me that

I would never walk again yet I walked out of the hospital and was home where I planned to stay. I began physical therapy with a local doctor and got better.

I knew I would not be doing stunt anymore and needed a change. I kept my weekend job at Corriganville but only did gun spinning acts and non-stunt rolls in the street shows, but I earned my ten dollars a weekend. I knew I was not going to get very far on that and was sick of eating Swanson chicken pot pies every day, so I started doing local gun shows to help make a buck.

At one of these shows I met fellow gun collector named Bob Romero and we became good friends. His dad Ray Romero was one of Hollywood's great make-up artists and the best hair men in the business (his specialty was mustaches and beards). At that time he was training Bob to take his make-up exam to become a make-up artist and Bob needed a dummy to practice on, so I volunteered.

We spent many long days in Ray's garage as he taught us the right way to do character make-up for motion pictures. Bob and I would take turns doing various make-up on each other. Ray was a good teacher and was hard on us when grading our work. For weeks we both sported burn marks on our faces from hot curling iron getting too close to the skin while curling beards or mustaches. Looking back it was all worth it for we became pretty good. Almost at once I knew I really like this new art I was learning and wanted to pursue it as a profession.

As the time grew close for the union to hold its testing for new make-up artists a lot of great make-up men helped us to prepare for the two day test. We spent days and some nights practicing our new found art; we would get friends to sit as models and did all sorts of crazy make-up on them. In those days make-up artists were really artists and craftsmen. We were taught every aspect of the make-up craft from beauty make-up to the art of making monsters.

We learned everything that might be needed on the set including the art of laying, hair strand by strand, to create mustaches, beards and sideburns. We were taught the art of creating appliances and prosthetic pieces to change the look of an actor into a famous person or alien. We perfected the art of character and old age make-up. We attended special classes in the art of creating the effects of bullet wounds, knife cuts, bruises, burns—just about anything a director could call for. While working on locations a make-up man had to be able to produce any effect that was called for from his make-up kit or magic box as some called it.

In those days we had no help from digital effects like those available today; we knew we had to produce it ourselves. Our teachers were hard on us for they wanted us to be the best, to take their place when the time came to carry on the tradition of excellent work that the great pioneers of Hollywood make-up had set before us. Many weeks were spent practicing and learning our craft with only a few hours of sleep.

Then came time to take the test! The test was held at Warner Brother's studio make-up department before a panel of older make-up men who really didn't want us young guys coming into the union and taking their jobs. The test consisted of every type of character make-up you can imagine and it had to be done in an allotted amount of time. It was then presented to the judges for examination, and they were hard to please. They nitpicked every detail of our work so we had to do everything right... it was grueling and the stress was unbelievable. We spent two very long days doing the best work we could turn out! At the end of the second day we were physically and mentally exhausted from the pressure.

To let off some steam and stress we all decided to go over to the Fog Cutter restaurant and bar and have a drink to celebrate making it through the exams. Well I'm not much of a drinker, but that night I started drinking mai tais. They were wet and cold and tasted great. After gulping down two very fast, I needed to hit the restroom so I took a big sip on my third one and headed for the short stairway leading to the pisser. That's all I remember until waking up in Las Vegas the next day at an old girlfriend's house. To this day I do not remember how I got there. I hate to think what an ass I must have made of myself on the plane and enroute to her house. I gave up drinking for a long time after that.

When I got back to Los Angeles, I learned that I had passed the make-up exam with flying colors. I was now on the auxiliary list with Local 706, the make-up union, and could work in the industry after all the group ones and twos were working. The big problem was almost all of the other people that passed the test were related to someone in the make-up industry and of course got hired first. It was almost unheard of in those days for an outsider to get work without help from a relative. I got a few small jobs here and there and then met Bill Tuttle who was the head of the MGM make-up department. He took a liking to me and I found a home at MGM and worked there for nearly fifteen years.

SAM PECKINPAH

We have all heard the stories of Sam Peckinpah, the drug and alcohol crazed genius with a death wish. Some called him Bloody Sam or the master of violence. Well that might all be true, but the Sam Peckinpah I knew was quite a different man. I can honestly say that I learned more about film making and respect and loyalty from him than anyone I ever worked with in the film industry. I found him to be brutally honest, loyal and a true friend who I still miss today.

Stories of my time working with Sam might sound crazy or unbelievable, but they are all true and I will tell them just as they happened.

I was a young make-up artist specializing in special effects back in 1968. I had worked on many films but had never been the department head (running the show). One afternoon my phone rang. It was Warner Brothers Studios requesting a meeting with me the next morning. I was very excited about this for I had never worked at Warners.

The next morning I arrived at the studio, the guard at the gate gave me directions to the make-up department and I drove in. The receptionist told me to go right in, that Mr. Bau was expecting me (Gordon Bau was the head of the make-up department). I was as excited as a kid at Christmas, this was my big chance to break into and work at Warners. I entered his office and right away I felt that something was wrong— Bau was very cold and just glared at me. His opening line was, "We don't appreciate politics here and don't like it one dammed bit. You young guys think you can cut the throats of the older make-up artists and get away with it. Well let me tell you, you'll never work at Warners if I have any say in it!" Needless to say I was taken aback, not expecting that type of reception.

Not being one who tolerates abuse of any kind I saw red. I looked him straight in the eye and said, "I don't know what you are talking about and don't really care. You have no reason to talk to me like that and I damn sure will not tolerate it. You can shove Warner Brothers up your ass if you are any example of the caliber of folks who work here." I was pretty pissed off.

As I turned to leave his office, he called me back, "Are you telling me that you didn't know that Sam Peckinpah requested you to work on his next film?" I told him I knew nothing about the film. I had only met Peckinpah once while working a few days on the "The Wild Bunch," and I was sure he would not remember me. He looked at me and saw that I was in no mood to listen to anymore of his bullshit. After a long silence he said, "They want to meet with you down in bungalow 234 on the back lot, my secretary will give you directions." I left his office without saying another word.

Making my way through the back lot to my mysterious meeting I cooled off a bit and thought, *Well, I guess I will never work on this lot, me and my big mouth blew it again.*

I entered the bungalow for the meeting and a secretary told me Sam was in a meeting. It would only be a few minutes, please have a seat. As I sat there I heard loud angry voices coming from Sam's office. All of a sudden the door burst open and a very angry man stormed out with Sam right on his heels. As the man left Sam shouted after him, "Fuck you!" He glared at me, then broke into a slight grin and said, "You're next, come on in!"

We entered his office and he said, "Who are you?" I told him and he asked me to tell him something about myself. I began naming all of the films and TV shows I had worked on, trying to make myself sound as important as I could. He looked me in the eye, "You know Stella Stevens has requested you on this film and Mr. Bau over in the make-up department is very pissed off and has told me that you will never work at Warner Brothers." I told him that I had just left Mr. Bau's office and had told him to stick Warners where the sun doesn't shine.

He broke into a big grin and said, "I like you, I want you on this film, I'll make a deal with you, if I ask you to do something and you tell me you can do it then screw it up, you will be on the first bus back to Hollywood, but if I ask you to do something and you tell me you will try, and then screw it up, you're safe." I told him that sounded like a fair deal to me. That is how my friendship with Sam started.

In a few weeks I arrived on location in the desert of Nevada near the Valley of Fire State Park, eighty miles north of Las Vegas in the middle of nowhere. The cast and crew were staying in a resort hotel owned by the state located on Lake Mead. It was off season and there was nothing there except us, a few coyotes and a lot of rattlesnakes.

As I was unpacking and getting the make-up department

set up, my phone rang, it was Bobby Visciglia prop man on the film. He said he needed to talk to me and would be at my room in a few minutes. When he showed up I thought he wanted to talk about the film, but He seemed nervous and told me that Sam had a problem and needed my help with something. Wanting to score points, I said sure I would be glad to help in any way I could. I will call you in a few minutes so get your case ready and wait for my call. He left. I thought that was a bit odd for it was nearly eleven o'clock in the evening. About twenty minutes later the phone rang. It was Bobby. He told me Sam had argued with his girlfriend and hit her. He needed me to do a little make-up job on her so they could get her out of the hotel past the night guard at the front desk. He said he would be down and tell me all about it.

When he showed up he seemed a bit spooked. "Listen," he said, "Sam hit his girlfriend and she fell and hit her head on a table and it killed her." They needed me to cover her wounds so they could get her out of the hotel, past the night guard and bury her in the desert before daylight. I thought, *Oh shit, oh Lord, what can I do?* I didn't want to get mixed up in a murder and cover up, but I was in a spot. Bobby told me that they would call me when the coast was clear to come down to Sam's room, knock twice and quickly come in. When he left I was a nervous wreck trying to find an excuse to not get involved in that mess, but I thought I would play it out and see what happened.

I got the call, grabbed my make-up case and headed to Sam's room and knocked twice as instructed. The door opened a bit and Bobby told me they had the lights off because there was a lot of blood and they were afraid if someone walked by they might see it. He told me to step in quickly and be quiet. I did as I was told and stood in the dark room not knowing what to expect.

Then I heard some faint snickers and chuckles. The lights came on and Sam and most of the crew were there hysterically laughing at me... It had all been a joke and a test to see if I was one of the gang. I guess I passed for after that Sam seemed to really like me. That is the way I started working on a film called "The Ballad of Cable Hogue" and began my long friendship with Sam Peckinpah.

The next morning was the first day of the shoot and my first day on our location site. The first day on location was always exciting because we would see where we would spend the next few weeks or months of our lives. I think everyone visualized what they thought the location and actors will look like when they read a script, and were anxious to see how close they were to the actual thing. When we left our hotel that morning at 3:30 a.m., we drove into the desert in the darkness of the pre-dawn morning. Some of us tried to catch a few extra hours of sleep on the ride but the rough dirt roads prevented that. As we drove through the desert and saw the sun rise, we began to realize just how far out in the middle of nowhere we were. We arrived at the location site and had our first look at our set. We found two small wood buildings joined together by a porch. That was Hogue's cabin where we would spend most of our time for the next few weeks, and what a time it was.

The cameras were set up and we started making movie magic. The first few days of shooting we spent in front of a Ritter wind fan creating sand and dust storms for the opening scenes of the movie. We would shoot till dark and sometimes later. By the time we made the long drive back to the hotel, most of us were worn out and ready for a hot bath and a warm bed!

However, there was that thing they called the Lizard Lounge, a bar within our hotel that Peckinpah had set up for the cast and crew—a place to blow off a little steam. The location was literally in the middle of nowhere and the nearest town, Las Vegas, was seventy-five miles away. So here we were stuck with a bunch of crazy wonderful Hollywood hard partiers and characters with nothing to do except to hang out at the Lizard Lounge and get crazy. I LOVED EVERY MINUTE OF IT! But it was pretty hard on a fellow's body.

Shooting "The Ballad of cable Hogue" was difficult. In the summertime our location reached over hundred and fifteen degrees in the shade, and there was no shade. The ground was so hot that at one point Bobby, our prop man, brought in ten gallon washtubs and filled them with water. We took turns standing in the water to keep the soles of our shoes from melting because of the hot ground. It became such a joke that Sam had a poster made that showed all the cast and crew standing on the rocks with shoes steaming, making it look like our feet were on fire. It seemed like the longer we spent in the desert the crazier things got. I think the combination of long hours working in the sun and long evenings and mornings at the Lizard Lounge started to take a toll on the crew. We were all totally physically and mentally worn out. Sometimes on the weekends some of the crew would go to Las Vegas to let off steam and relax a bit. Most of the time we spent at the hotel resting, trying to get back to normal and ready for Monday morning shooting.

One morning we were on location ready to work. We waited for a couple hours but no one showed up, Sam, Jason Robards and our prop man were all missing. We sat around for close to three hours waiting for our leaders. We had no idea what was going on so we just waited. Finally we spotted a black limousine kicking up a cloud of dust as they neared our location. We all knew that the men in the black suits from the main office were descending on us and that was not a good sign. They roared up in front of the crew, stopped their car and called a production meeting right there in the middle of the desert. They proceeded to tell us that Sam, Jason and Bobby had gotten drunk in Ely, Nevada, shot up a whore house and were all in jail. Needless to say, that day was pretty much of a waste of time, but late that afternoon Sam and the others returned and it was back to work again.

It's hard to explain to someone what being on a distant location is like, it's just a different world with different values and life styles. We would work our asses off for hours then have a POV (Point of View) change and camera move that could take up to three or more hours to set up. During these set up changes some members of the crew would take naps, read or play cards to kill time.

Not me! I would explore, look for things. I learned the first day on location that there were Indian artifacts strewn all over the hills surrounding us, and that is where I would head. I spent many wonderful hours wandering those hills looking for lost treasures left by Native Americans and found quite a few.

A funny thing happened one day as I was searching the hills. I am always in a sort of a trance when concentrating on the ground looking for arrowheads and other odd shapes, pretty much oblivious to anything around me. One day I heard something behind me and turned around to find three men dressed in black uniforms pointing machine guns at me and looking not a bit friendly.

"What are you doing here?" they demanded. As soon as I got my heart out of my throat I told them that I was working with the movie crew and was taking a walk in the desert while the next shot was being set up. "Did you know that you are in a government restricted area and could be shot for trespassing?"

I assured them that I did not. I was taken to a large black military vehicle and returned to our location site. When we arrived the officer in charge had Sam call everyone together. He proceeded to tell us that the hills east of us were government restricted lands and none of us were to go near them. It seems I had wandered into Area 13 or the Groom Lake area and that was a no no! After all they didn't want any UFO aliens abducting me and doing experiments on me … Shit! I didn't either.

Another funny thing happened while we were in the Valley of Fire location. We were preparing to film the scene where Cable Hogue has Taggert and Bowen (L.Q. Jones and Strother Martin) cornered in a hole they had dug looking for Hogue's hidden money. Sam had told them to get down in the hole and not to look over the top till he called for action.

What he did not tell them was that he had brought a rattlesnake wrangler in with boxes full of very large diamond

back rattlers (all had their mouths sewn shut so they could not bite). Sam gave our cameraman the silent sign to roll the cameras, at the same time he signaled the snake wrangler to start tossing the snakes into the hole. The first snake slid into the hole and another and another. L.Q. took one look at what was happening and made one mighty leap out of the hole and went after Peckinpah cursing him for every kind of a son of a bitch he could come up with … Sam loved it, he ran away laughing. He thought it was great fun.

Meanwhile, poor Strother was still in the hole swarming with snakes. He looked like a cartoon character, his feet and legs were going a mile a minute but all he was doing was kicking up loose sand and made no progress. It was a funny sight and everyone was having a good laugh except poor ole Strother who kept murmuring, "Oh my Lord, help me. Help me!"

Finally Sam called, "Cut," and they got him out of the hole and calmed him down. That was the type of thing Sam loved to do to his actors to get an honest reaction from them. Everyone knew if Sam liked you, that sooner or later he was going to screw with you, and it would be your turn in the barrel.

After many weeks of very hard work and long hours, we finished our work at that location site. We moved to Apache Junction, Arizona, to film the interior and town scenes for the picture. It was a nice change. We were back in civilization in a nice hotel with real restaurants and things to do and see. It was like being released from prison. Our shooting location was a western town set built just outside of town at the base of the Superstition Mountains. We started the shoot and everything seemed to be going well. The days were hot which made shooting inside a bit harder. At times the temperature on the sets rose to one hundred and ten degrees and more because of the big arc lights used to light the sets. It made my job as a make-up artist much more difficult. The mustaches and make-up tend to melt off at those temperatures.

I had been having some back problems from an old stunt injury and was taking Valium and Darvon to ease the pain.

I was a bit out of sorts but trying my best to keep on top of things. One day while shooting inside the small Wells Fargo office with actor R.G. Armstrong, it was exceptionally hot and I was having a pretty bad day with my back, but doing my job as a make-up artist trying to keep R.G.'s make-up together. I would go in between shots and do what needed to be done to get him ready for the next take.

The cinematographer on this shoot was one that Sam used on most of his films, Lucian Ballard. He was truly one of the greats; he created the look on the Wild Bunch and now on Cable Hogue. He always carried a riding crop or stick while shooting; I guess it was part of his image. He was old Hollywood and played the role to the hilt mixed with a large dose of ego. While I was working on R.G. between shots I heard someone shout, "Hey what are you doing on my set?" Well I thought someone from the public had wandered onto the set so paid no attention. "I mean you, you big dumb son of a bitch," and he jabbed me hard in the back with his stick.

It hurt like the dickens. I immediately saw red and before thinking, jerked the stick from his hand and snapped it over his head. The set went dead silent. After the shock had worn off Lucian screamed, "You're fired. You'll never work in Hollywood again. Get off my set!"

Trying to calm down a bit I looked him in the eye and said, "Fuck you. Stick your set up your pompous ass. I quit!" I stormed off the set, crossed the street to the make-up department and began packing my gear. I had calmed down a bit when my good friend, Stella Stevens, came in and asked what had happened. I told her what had just taken place and that I had been fired.

About that moment Sam came into the room glaring at me. I thought, *Oh great now Sam is going to read me the riot act.* We stood staring at each other for a few seconds then he said, "You know what I was thinking while watching what happened?"

I said, "I can only imagine."

He broke into one of those Peckinpah sly grins and said, "I was thinking cut, print, cut, print. Now come on back over to the set. Lucian owes you an apology and he's going to do it in front of the whole crew."

"I don't think that's ever going to happen," I said.

"Well by God he'll be on the next bus back to Hollywood if it doesn't. You were doing your job and he was showing off for the public. Come on."

I thought, *What the hell this should be interesting,* so we went back across the street to the set.

As we entered the set all eyes were on us and you could have heard a pin drop. Lucian screamed, "Get him off my set!"

"You owe this man an apology," Sam said, "He was doing his job and you were wrong!"

"Like hell I do," Lucian replied. Sam looked at him "You will apologize or you'll be on the next bus back to Hollywood."

"I will not do it," he said. Sam's eyes went cold as he gave Lucian one of his looks. "You would fire me?"

"You know I will. Now apologize to the man!"

I guess I should not have been grinning but I could not help it, I was enjoying watching Lucian squirm. I heard a faint, "I'm sorry," come from Lucian and thought it was all done with.

"That won't do. Say it so everyone can hear!"

"I'm sorry" he said much louder this time.

"Okay, let's get back to work" Sam said. "We're making a picture here."

And we all went back to work. Needless to say, Lucian and I had a very uneasy working relationship from then on. It seemed like every time I worked for Sam, someone was always firing me for one reason or another. There is one thing I can say about Sam Peckinpah, if you were in the right he would always come through for you no matter who or what the situation. It is one of the reasons I always respected the man.

Towards the end of shooting "The Ballad of Cable Hogue," Sam announced that he was going to run the director's final cut of "The Wild Bunch" Sunday at a local theatre the studio had rented. We were all invited to join him if we would like to see the film. Most of the crew and cast showed up for the screening. Most of us had no idea what we were about to see. Sam had been working on his final cuts of the film as we were shooting "Cable Hogue" and this was the result.

As the lights went down and the screen flickered to life I don't think any of us were prepared for what we were about to witness. After nearly four hours we walked out of the theatre, most of us in a state of awe or shock. We had never seen a film like "The Wild Bunch" with its inner cutting and slow motion violence. For me it was one of the greatest films I had ever seen, I knew then I was working for one of Hollywood's real geniuses… It made me proud!

We finished shooting "Cable Hogue" a few days later.

After working on one of Sam's films it always took weeks to rest up and to get back to a normal and feel human again. The long hours, little sleep and endless partying and abuse takes its toll on the body even when you're young.

Sam called one day and wanted me bring my throwing knives to his house. I had taught him the art of knife and tomahawk throwing while we were filming "Cable Hogue." When I arrived at his house Emilio Fernandez, Warren Oats, and R.G. Armstrong were all there and very drunk. Sam wanted me to show them how to throw a knife and had made a bet with them that I could hit any target they wanted to put up.

After hitting a few of their targets, Warren stepped up and announced that he was going to hold up a wooden block and wanted me to throw a knife at it while he held it. I drew the line there and made some lame excuse for not doing it.

I guess that leads up to something I want to relate, a little insight into Sam and his odder side. Every time Sam rented an office after I taught him how to throw a knife, he had the studio install a sheet of five eighths inch plywood to the back of his office door. Many times you could hear the steady thump of the throwing knives I gave him hitting the door as he practiced and let off a little steam… He became pretty good!

THE GETAWAY

A few months passed and I received a call to come to a production meeting to discuss a new film Sam was starting called "The Getaway" starring Steve McQueen and Ali McGraw. After we had agreed on rates and discussed the special make-up effects that were needed in the film, I gathered supplies and equipment for the job. I had nearly a month lead time before I was to report to Texas to begin filming, plenty of time for what I needed to do. A couple of weeks before my start date I got a call from Sam telling me to come to Texas now! I was surprised because my start date was weeks away. I ask him if they had moved the start date up or what was going on. He told me to not worry about it, I was on salary starting today, just get my ass down there right away.

I was in San Marquis, Texas the next morning and reported to the production office to find out what the big rush was all about. Sam asked me if I could drive a car with stick shift. I assured him that I could. "See that gray Falcon in the parking lot?" he said. "Well your job will be to take it, pick up Ali McGraw every morning, and teach her how to drive it. We start shooting in two weeks."

I was just handed a Peckinpah favor and a great job. Ali and I sat down with a map of the area and drew a one hundred mile circle around San Marquis, every day we headed off in a different direction exploring the many small towns in the area. We had a great time, all on the studio, and Ali learned to drive a stick shift. Sam always did things to put a few extra bucks in your pocket if he liked you.

The first day shooting "The Getaway" started with a bang. Sam would be filming one of the show's big special effects scenes, blowing up a hay truck and setting a barn on fire. In the script, that would act as a diversion to the bank robbery by McQueen.

I think most of the town had shown up to watch the fireworks, even the local fire department was there standing by. I had nothing to do because there were no actors working that day so I was also an observer (also thought this would be a good place to get a look at the locals… Girls!!!).

Everything was ready. Sam called action and all hell broke loose. The truck exploded in a huge ball of flames and everyone dove for cover. It blew out the side of the barn and it also exploded in flames. The local fire department immediately rushed in with sirens screaming and red lights flashing, right into the middle of Sam's shot. I knew this was not going to be pretty, but I knew the show was about to start.

Sam leaped off the Chapman crane, running toward them screaming at the top of his lungs. He called them everything except a white man. The First Ad was also screaming at the firemen to get there asses out of the shot. Sam finally caught one, pointed at the camera and screamed something I could not hear. After that it did not take long for the firemen to get out of the scene. Sam walked back to the Chapmen, got on it so all could see and raised the one finger salute to all!

Well, that's how the first day's shooting went, almost everything we did was screwed up one way or the other. I guess that set the tone for the second day of shooting…not one of my shining moments.

The second day's location site was in a pretty nice area with all the location trailers arranged in two rows facing each other. The make-up trailer was right across from Ali and Steve's personal motor homes. I had never met Steve McQueen and was looking forward to meeting and working with him. I had enjoyed his work in films for years. When he arrived on set he had a few buddies with him and they went directly into his motor home. I waited a few minutes and went across and knocked on his door, it was answered by his personal driver and cook, Jimmy Jeminez. I introduced myself and ask to speak to Mr. McQueen about his make-up requirements. Steve shouted for me to come in. We talked for a while about some of the special effect make-up that needed to be done later in the film.

We finished our conversation and I saw that his cook had prepared a huge plate of huevos rancheros and he was about to have his breakfast. I excused myself and told him that when he was ready, I would be right across way in the make-up trailer and started to leave. He began to eat his breakfast and between bites said, "Do it now!" I explained that I could not do his make-up while he was eating and without lights in his motor home and started to leave again. He jumped up and shouted at me, "I said I wanted you to do my make-up now!"

I tried again to explain in a gentlemanly manner why I could not and would not do it under those circumstances. He started poking me in the chest with his finger and getting very vocal and angry. Now I am normally a real easy going, hard to rile up, type of a guy, but I really don't like someone verbally abusing me and damn sure won't put up with some two-bit actor poking me in the chest while he is doing it.

I was very cool not wanting this thing to get any bigger than it was. I told Steve to stop poking me and calm down. Well he poked me even harder, I guess showing off for his buddies. I told him he had one more poke. He asked, "Or what?"

"Or I'll knock you on your ass," I said before thinking. Well he poked me even harder the next time. I saw red and bitch slapped him across the face (didn't want to bruise or cut him because it would cause problems for make-up). My slap sat him down in his chair and left a big red hand print across his face…I left.

I walked to the make-up trailer and I, and everyone else within ear-shot, heard him screaming that I was fired and my make-up career was over, that I would never work in Hollywood again. Damn fired on a Peckinpah film again and on the second day of filming, that's a record for me. I figured that I was a goner for sure. After all I had bitch slapped one of Hollywood's biggest stars and the star of this film. I stared packing up my supplies and equipment knowing any minute Sam or the First Ad would burst through the door and fire my big ass.

Well the door burst opened and it was Ali. She had heard what happened and came over to hear my side of the story. After she listened, she asked me not to leave yet and said she would be right back. In a few minutes she returned with Sam. "Where the fuck do you think you're going?" he asked. I told him my story. Told him that Steve had fired me so I was going home.

He looked me in the eye, as only Sam could do and said, "He can't fire you. I hired you and I'm the only one that can fire you and you aren't fired." He grinned. "There's been many times I wanted to smack him myself, now go get him ready to shoot." I told Sam that I would not work on him, that he would have to bring in another make-up man to do his make-up on this film. Sam asked me if I would do it just today and they would have another make-up man here tomorrow. I refused and told him that I was afraid if I did his make-up and he smarted off to me or pushed me again, I might hurt him. Sam smiled as he shouted, "We shoot only long shots today." I think Sam always got kicks from anyone who stood up and did not take any BS from the so called elite of Hollywood.

I guess I am a bit of an asshole at times for almost every day after that I made a point to say, "Good Morning" to Steve, just to let him know I was still there.

I must say that later in the film Steve came over and apologized for what had happened between us. He explained that he was going through a rough divorce and was under a lot of stress. We shook hands and actually  became pretty good friends on and off the set. I think it takes a real man to stand up and say he's wrong and I think Steve McQueen was one.

Another funny thing that happened with Steve was one night most of the crew had gone out to dinner at a local steak house a few miles from our hotel. For weeks Steve had been on transportation to get him a better car to drive while on location, but all they could come up with was a new four door Ford (not a bad car but definitely not a McQueen vehicle). After we had finished our meal, Steve asked me if I wanted a ride back to the hotel for we had a very early call the next morning. We hopped into the car and were off. Steve was not happy with this car and began cursing it as we drove down the long road home.

The hotel where we were staying was on a golf course and the road leading to the hotel was straight through the middle of it. Steve looked over at me with a big grin on his face and asked if I could swim. I told him I could and ask him why he wanted to know. "I'm about to get a new car," he answered and veered off the road straight into a pond on the golf course. The car went airborne, splashed into the pond and sunk to the bottom. Luckily it was only a few feet deep so there was no real danger. Steve was laughing crazily, "I bet they get me a better car tomorrow," he said. We splashed our way out of the pond and walked a few hundred yards back to the hotel. The next day Steve had a new car.

We stayed at a great hotel called the Aquarena Hotel and Resort built right on a beautiful fresh water spring. My room was great. It had a balcony that overlooked the main spring, and one could dive from the balcony into the water below.

My room had everything going for it except one thing. Al Lettiri and Sally Strothers had the room right next to mine and every night they would damn near knock the wall in frolicking in their bed. At first I was alarmed and thought they were having a knockdown, drag out fight, but then realized they were just in love and doing what lovers do... Damn, I didn't know such a little gal could make that much noise! I ask Al to move the bed to the other side of the room, which he did... Problem solved.

As on all Peckinpah films there was some crazy shit that went on all the time. Someone may get a kick out of these stories.

One of the things I found funny happened as we were filming the bank robbery and getaway. In one scene Steve and Ali were escaping in the old Ford and were to lose control of the car and smash it through the porch of a nearby house and continue out of town. Well the day we were shooting that scene most of the town gathered to watch the filming. Steve was always aware of the fans and knew his reputation as a great driver that does all of his own stunts.

When it was time to do some run-throughs for camera angles and special effects, Steve and Ali got into the Ford and made a big entrance so all could see. Steve drove the car through its paces up to the point where the crash and stunt were to happen, returned to where Sam was watching, and loudly ask him if that was okay or did he need another run (most of this was played to the crowd). Sam said, "Let's roll camera on the next pass. Everyone this will be a take."

At that point Steve gunned the car into the alley behind the house, and Gary Combs (Steve's double) got into the driver's seat and roared out the other end of the alley. He pulled to the start point, Sam called for "Action" and off Gary went, cashing through the porch, through a big ball of flames and landing right on his mark. A perfect take! Gary does not stop but roars into the alley again. Steve quickly takes his place behind the wheel, emerges from the alley and pulls up to Sam. He gets out brushing himself off … "How was that Sam?" he asked.

The crowd clapped and cheered. They thought they had just seen Steve McQueen do one of his own stunts when what they had seen was the old smoke and mirror gag.

Another bit of information or trivia you might like is this. The next time you watch "The Getaway" and see the scene I just wrote about, watch the background crowds to see if you recognize anyone. If you look closely you might see James Garner grinning at you. He had just delivered a custom van to a buddy of his who was working on the film, so Sam put him in the film as an extra.

We finished our shooting in San Marquis and moved down the border to El Paso. Our main location or set was an old rundown hotel right on the border. The production company had rented a building from the city for almost nothing, for after we finished our shooting it was to be demolished and a newer building would replace it. That meant Sam could blow the thing apart or just shoot it up and there was no limit—anything he wanted to do was fine. Our production offices were set up on the main floor or lobby of an old hotel, everything ran out of there. We stayed at a nearby hotel that had a nice swimming pool area on its roof, this was our Lizard Lounge in El Paso. Every evening and Sunday mornings we had food catered, strawberries and champagne flowed freely along with some south-of-the-border weed.

It was pretty crazy at times but as I remember it, I think it was fun. The late hours and partying kept us pretty worn out and tired. Well Sam took care of that for us. Every morning we lined up and got a vitamin B-12 shot and a cross-top tablet (uppers to some folks) from the medic on set. I must say it sure did get one up and going for most of the day.

As you might have guessed by now most all of us, cast and crew, were consuming more than our share of the local grown magical weed. Things were getting pretty tight and our supplies were getting low to the point that some were going into the panic mode. We should all have known better, the border was only a few steps away from our location and we had a lot of locals working on the film. One of our extras set up a deal to buy weed across the border and at a very good price. The problem was how to get it across the border without getting caught. A very clever, even genius, plan was formulated that we thought would work, at least we hoped it would.

The next day we were filming a scene where Slim Pickens was taking building supplies (scrap tin siding and junk) across the border to Chawa Chawa City. We were shooting at a small border checkpoint and the studio had made arrangements to allow Slim to drive back and forth across the border for the scene. Well every time he crossed into Mexico, there would be eight or nine pounds of marijuana hidden under the junk in the back of the truck and brought into the good old USA. At the end of the shooting at this location we had over forty pounds of marijuana stored in the production office, praise God! We were saved, we had done it, we had become international drug smugglers, my mom would have been real proud of her number one son! I must say that my old friend, Slim Pickens, had no idea what was going on, and had no part in it.

The next day we were to start shooting the big hotel shootout, the climax of the film and Sam's big day to do what he does best—blow things up and kill people. When I arrived at the set that morning, there were lots of people standing around the old hotel, some watching, some working. I noticed numerous city police and a few Texas Rangers and was hit with the distinctive smell of marijuana reeking from the building. I panicked a bit and rushed into Gordie Dawson's office and told him that one could smell marijuana all the way down the block and there were police and rangers outside. He told me not to worry. It had all been taken care of, and there was no problem. It always amazed me what money could buy and what movie folks could get away with!!!! The crew and cast were very mellow for the rest of the shoot. As all old hippies know, a few hits on a joint sure takes the edge off things!

We finished the principle shooting on "The Getaway" a few weeks later.

Another Peckinpah story happened in Mexico City while

LAST SHOOTING "THE GETAWAY"

filming at the Churubusco Studios. I was working on a film called "The Hand" starring my good friend Samantha Eggars. It was a pretty silly story about a severed hand that ran around killing folks, but it was a chance to spend some time in Mexico and an easy job, so I went for it. I had lived in Guadalajara, Mexico for a few years and grew to love the country and its people. It was also a great place to hunt for antique firearms to add to my collection.

At the Churubusco Studio's most of the sound stages were built with adobe bricks with a dirt floor. We filmed in one that had a large hole dug into the floor and made it into a torture chamber. It was very dark on the stage with the exception of torches burning inside the torture chamber. I was talking with Samantha near the edge of the hole when all of a sudden I was pushed into it. I went ass over tea kettle into the pit. Fortunately I had worked as a stunt man for a few years and knew how to take a fall.

I got to my feet brushed myself off and became aware of someone hysterical laughing at the edge of the hole above me. I was pretty ticked off and headed right for the laughing jackass, not knowing who it was or why I had been pushed into the hole. I saw a very drunk Sam Peckinpah and Emilio Fernandez who could barely stand, having a good laugh at me. Sam rushed to me, threw his arm around me and said something like, "Where the fuck were you on my last film?" (I had missed working on "Osterman Weekend" because of some studio politics and a First Ad who did not like me). I told him why I missed his last shoot. He grumbled something about the front office and the assholes we all had to work with and invited me to have lunch with him and Emilo at the studio commissary. I told him that I would join them as soon as we broke for lunch.

The commissary was bustling with people and at first I did not see Sam, then I heard someone call my name. He was sitting at Emilio's reserved table in the corner of the room. It was no ordinary table; it was on a platform three feet above the floor. I found out later that Emilio had it built so he could survey the room looking for pretty senoritas … He was quite a big star and celebrity in his country and loved the ladies.

As soon as I sat down, Sam poured me a double shot of

tequila in a tall glass... "Well Doctor, (Sam called everybody Doctor) what the hell are you doing down here?" I told him about the turkey I was working on and we both had a good laugh.

Emilo said, "Sam, give him a lottery ticket, we all win some money."

Sam started to hand me a ticket, then drew it back... "I'll give you one better." He quickly scribbled something on the ticket then handed it to me saying "I owe you one plus." On the front of the lottery ticket he had written

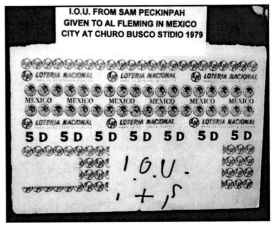

"I owe you one plus" and signed it with his SP brand. I framed that ticket and it hangs on my wall just under an eleven by fourteen portrait of Sam that I took while filming "The Ballad of Cable Hogue."

As I said before, Sam was a very interesting character and under all that rough exterior lurked a very lovable, kind man. I feel really privileged to have known him and called him my friend. I miss him to this day! I know it sounds like I am praising the man or putting him upon a pedestal. Maybe I am, but we all have people who come into our lives and make a difference. Well Sam was one of those special people in my life! I know he was flawed in many ways and the alcohol and drugs were eating him up, but still he made a difference. I learned many things about life from Sam, some good and some bad. I was enriched knowing him.

There was a script called "The Cossack and the Cowboy" that Sam told me he always wanted to do more than any he had. A funny story about that elusive script happened at Warren Oats' log house in Montana.

I got a call from my good friend, Slim Pickens, inviting me to come down to Warren's place for a little get-together with Sam and Warren, a party barbecue. Well, how could I say no to an invite like that? I left my ranch in Kalispell, Montana and headed to Warren's. Slim met me at the gate and told me there was a very serious poker game going on up at the house. Ben Johnson showed up with a script that both Sam and Warren really wanted to do "The Cossack and the Cowboy," and they had been playing for most of the night to see who would end up owning the project.

We entered the house and it was obvious that everyone was feeling no pain and was deep into the game. Slim and I entered the room and Sam called a stop to the game and announced that it was time to eat. He came up to me and whispered in my ear, "These assholes are beating me to death. You came just in time." Warren had a few locals barbecuing some great elk steaks in the backyard so we all sat and chowed down. Of course the tequila flowed freely. At the end of our meal we sat back and exchanged some great stories (wish I had had a recorder). I don't remember most of them. Two days later I bid them good bye.

Slim told me later that nobody knew who ended up owning the script, everyone thought they owned it... Funny thing is that even today the true ownership of "The Cossack and the Cowboy" is in question. It is a shame for Sam would have made a great motion picture out of it!

That was the last time I saw Sam, he passed away a few months later.

FUNNY HAPPENING

In 1966 I was called to do some screen tests at Universal Studios with actor Paul Newman for a film called "Torn Curtain." Mr. Newman had taken a pretty nasty motorcycle crash and had road rash all down his left arm. The test was to see if make-up could hide this area enough that the camera could not see it...The test and film was directed by legendary director, Alfred Hitchcock. The tests went fine, everything looked good, and everyone seemed happy.

The make-up department in those days was in the back of the studio, and each morning I had to make the long walk past stages and production offices to get there. Mr. Hitchcock's office was on my route. It was painted white with two pillars on each side of his large office window. That morning I noticed him standing looking out his window. As I passed by he gave me a long stare, then slowly gave me the finger, that's right the old bird, the one finger salute, I got flipped off by Alfred Hitchcock... I couldn't believe it. That happened every morning as I passed his window, and you know he never cracked a smile or even acknowledge it.

The last day of the test shooting my girlfriend wanted to meet Mr. Newman so I brought her with me. As we walked to the make-up department I made sure I pointed out Mr. Hitchcock's office. Sure enough there he was, and like it was planned, as we passed up came the finger to a rigid salute.

Before I could stop her, she gave him a dirty look and flipped him off. That was the only time I ever saw Mr. Hitchcock laugh, and he seemed to really enjoy it. I hustled her down the walkway to safety. "I'm glad it's the last day of shooting, for I'm a goner for sure," I told her. She got to meet Mr. Newman.

Hitchcock never said a word about what happened, just gave me a wink and said, "Nice girlfriend you have there!" So everything turned out okay in the end. I must hold some kind of record, being flipped off by Alfred Hitchcock every morning before going to work... How many people can say that? OH HOLLYWOOD, AIN'T IT GREAT?

BURNT OFFERINGS

In 1966 I found myself at Twentieth Century Fox studio doing make-up tests on actress Bette Davis for the upcoming film "Burnt Offerings." I had never met Miss Davis before doing the tests but had always admired her work.

The initial meeting went fine. She informed me that she wanted the cheapest liquid paint type make-up from the five and ten cent store. I told her that she could have the best products made for our budget was quite large. She stopped me in mid-sentence and told me that she wanted exactly what she had just told me. She wanted... So that's what I got!!! She was a tough old broad, knew exactly what she wanted and would accept nothing less. I really respected her and her spunk. She was a real card and one of Hollywood's great.

In a few days we left for our location in Oakland,

TV GUIDE SHOOT

California. It turned out to be one of the strangest films I ever worked on. I must tell you that everything written here is the honest truth. I have not made anything up!

First I should tell you something about the cast of characters in this tale.

- Oliver Reed. Drug crazed alcoholic lunatic, and wanted to be macho mad man.
- Bette Davis. Great Actress and star. Wanted to be treated like it is still the 1950s.
- Karen Black…Looney Tune.
- Burgess Meredith…Certifiably crazy.
- And our director, Dan Curtis…Wanted to out-macho everyone on the set. Ego maniac but good director.

So there you have it, a cast of crazies and they were all mine for the duration of the show, at least most were.

The first day on location I received a phone call from Oliver Reed inviting me to go out to dinner to get to know each other (I had never met him). We met at the arranged time and took two limousines to a restaurant called the Rusty Pelican on the bay in Oakland. There were eight in our party, Oliver, his girlfriend, Reggie, his body guard, and the rest were members of the film crew.

We were seated and Oliver informed us that it was customary for new friends to share wine before eating and that all bottles must be empty before ordering dinner. Wine was brought to the table, I should say, lots of wine was brought to the table, and not wanting to offend our host we drank it!

We began our meal at the salad bar, most of us were feeling no pain and in a jolly mood. As we worked our way through the various selections offered for salad we each took what we wanted and moved to the next item. Oliver was in front of me and taking a long time making his choices so I stepped around him to the next item. He grabbed me by the arm and told me that was rude, then from nowhere slapped me in the face. I was stunned at first, then smacked him back, he slapped me again I smacked him again. We must have looked like the three stooges minus one standing there slapping each other like clowns. Finally Reggie rushed in and ended our little slapping match.

I must admit I was a bit pissed off. Oliver slapped me on the back and said, "I like you Yank!" Thinking back I don't know if that was a good thing or a curse… Anyway we became friends and the lunacy began.

Our location was a large Victorian mansion on a large wooded estate in old Oakland, California. We were pretty much secluded when we entered the gate and in a world all of our own, in other words it was a Looney Bin. We were all assigned rooms upstairs. My make-up room was right at the head of the winding stairway at the top of the stairs.

The first day of shooting we had an early call at 4:30 a.m. It was a cold damp morning. As I climbed the stairs I was hit with a bucket of ice water from above and greeted with a roar of laughter from Oliver who thought that was great sport. I thought, *So this is how it was to be, ole Oliver likes to play practical jokes!* Revenge is sweet, so I bided my time, and that afternoon I struck back! While Oliver was filming a scene, I crept into his room and cut one side of the zipper on his pants and contact cemented his shoes to the floor and waited.

I knew he liked to get back to the hotel and the bar quickly after they called a wrap on the set, and sure enough he came in a rush. I made small talk while he changed. He pulled on his pants and zipped them up and then tried to zip them again before he realized something was wrong. He caught on, looked at me and grinned. "You got me Yank!" he said. He slipped into his shoes and almost did an endo for they were glued solidly to the floor. "Damn Yank, you got me again!" I smiled and reminded him that he had started it. I must say he took it in good spirits and seemed to enjoy it. That started a game that got crazier as the filming went on.

For some reason Oliver always seemed to be testing himself and his manliness. One day he challenged me to arm wrestling contest which we did and I beat him without too much trouble. From that day on whenever there was someone around or when he had an audience he would challenge me again, and I would beat him again. I could see that it was getting to him a bit and thought he would finally get the message, but not Oliver, he was determined to beat me. After weeks of this foolishness Reggie called me to the side and told me to let him win once and it would all stop. I did and sure enough it all stopped.

Shooting proceeded and we got into the special effects part of the filming where the house would shed its shingles and have other special effects. There were long hours of down time while the effects crew rigged the house. To help pass the time we formed football teams, our director had Curtis Crushers and Ollie had Reeds Raiders. We had some

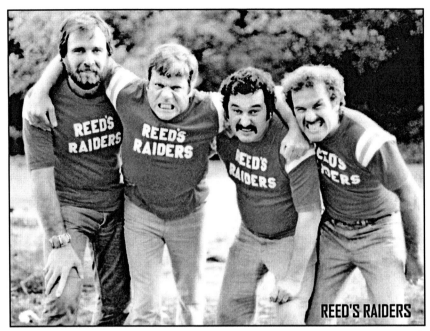

REED'S RAIDERS

pretty rough and tumble games on the front lawn of the old mansion. Oliver and Curtis tried to out-macho each other.

It got really crazy around the middle of shooting. Oliver heard that Richard Harris was shooting a film in San Francisco and that started what I called total madness. One must remember that Harris was an Irishman and Oliver was English and both had the tough guy image! Now this will sound completely crazy, but it is absolutely true. They started sending threatening notes to each other, challenging the other to a duel, or a boxing match, then the death threats started. It was total madness. It would have been funny, but they were both serious! From what I was told they had bad blood between them from a past experience. At one point the police got involved and paid Oliver a visit on the set. After a long interview with him, they left and the craziness seemed to stop, or so we all thought.

One afternoon we arrived back at our hotel and were met by four British soldiers in full red dress uniforms wearing large bear skin helmets, beating drums and marching led by a regimental band leader. What a sight it was! Oliver got out of the limousine and the leader came to attention and saluted Oliver who returned his salute. Oliver was all smiles as he turned and said, "What do you think lads?" *Hell, what could we think? Except this asshole is crazy!* This parade of fools followed Oliver wherever he went for the next week. It seems that Oliver had sent for them to come over to be his personal bodyguards because he knew it would get back to Harris and piss him off again. Oh, I forgot to mention that these proper English soldier lads all liked to tip the old bottle, so they fit right in with all the craziness.

One night after all the bars had closed and Oliver and the boys had on a pretty good glow, Oliver had the great idea that we should play a war game he called The Brits challenge the Colonials (the driver and me being the Colonials). It was after two in the morning when Ollie had the driver stop in a wooded rural high dollar estate section of old Oakland. "Everybody out," he ordered, "We will give you colonials a good head start then we will come and hunt you down." I tried to explain to him that this was not a good idea, that these estates had alarms and some had dogs patrolling the ground. Someone could get hurt.

I knew my protests were in vain, but I had to try. The driver looked at me with a look on his face that let me know he wanted no part of this ridiculous game but didn't know how to get out of it. "Come on," I said and jumped the stone wall of the estate. Once inside I told him, "We will hide amongst the trees and when they wander off into the darkened woods, we will go back to the car and wait for them to return." We did.

We could hear them crashing and stumbling through the woods, Oliver shouting orders to his drunken troops, a fool leading his fools. This went on for some time. It was quite a funny sight—four British soldiers in beautiful red dress uniforms falling blindly, cursing, thrashing about in the woods taking orders from Oliver, or should I say General

Reed. I noticed that they were nearing the main house on the estate and knew that was not good… Before I could do anything about it, the security lights came on illuminating the entire outside of the house and the owner came out with a shotgun pointed right at Oliver. "What the hell is going on out here and who are you?" he demanded. It was amazing to see how fast Oliver changed from a raving drunk to a proper English gentleman. He introduced himself to the man who did not seem impressed at all, and explained that he was rehearsing for a scene in his latest movie.

The owner was pretty pissed off and was having none of this foolishness. "This is private property and you are all trespassing, I have called the police!"

Like a well-timed scene in a movie, the Oakland police arrived guns drawn and in a foul mood. The driver and I watched from afar as the scene played itself out. If I only had a camera—there was Oliver and the Brits with hands in the air at gun point. We approached the scene thinking we might be able to help straighten out the situation being that we were good old American boys. As we approached one of the cops pointed his gun at us also.

Oliver came to the rescue. He was wearing a very expensive Rolex watch which he took off and handed to the property owner. "Here this will make up for any inconvenience we have caused you. We did not mean any harm. We were just having a bit of fun." Of course the watch was accepted and all was forgiven and there were no charges filed.

I know you must think that had to have been a made-up story, as crazy as it seems, but it is one hundred percent true.

Things calmed down a bit. I was a good boy, no more long nights drinking and partying. I limited myself to go out with the group only on weekends.

Some of the crew were invited to join Oliver and his crowd for a dinner party at the Rusty Pelican restaurant on the bay in Oakland. After a great dinner and too many bottles of wine and alcohol Oliver suggested that we move the party to his suite of rooms at the hotel. When we arrived back at his suite, we entered his room and being the nosy type, I spied three swords sitting in one corner of the room that Oliver had used in the film "The Three Musketeers" and asked Oliver if I could have a look at them. BIG MISTAKE! When I picked one up and was examining it, I heard from behind me, "On Guard!" I turned around and found Oliver standing at the ready position with his sword pointing at me.

"Defend yourself," he shouted as he lunged at me with his sword.

Fortunately I had trained with swords and was able to parry his thrust and avoid his charge. He grew even more aggressive and continued his attack in earnest. Everyone in the room stopped what they were doing and watched in amazement at what was taking place. I called to Oliver to stop, that this was getting out of hand, but nothing got through… He had turned into d'Artagnan or some other drunken swordsman he had once played in a movie.

As I defended myself, one parry with my sword accidentally nicked his cheek and drew blood which combined with his sweating quickly looked much worse than it actually was. He turned into a raving lunatic and really tried to kill me. Everyone in the room yelled at him to stop. Reggie tried to get control of the crazy drunken fool, but nothing worked!

Zing the sword just missed me and hit the wall causing a large gash. Clang, clang, the noise of our swords echoed through the room, as the people moved out of danger. I was literally fighting for my life, I thought, *I have to do something quick or this crazy bastard is going to kill me.* About that time he caught me across the knuckles with his sword causing a pretty good cut. It must have been quite a site, sweat mixing with our blood; we looked a mess. Oliver's shirt was soaked with blood and sweat and my sleeve was a bright red color from my bleeding knuckles.

I had an idea of how I could stop the madness. If I could get to the door, I could quickly step out in the hallway, make it to my room and step inside. Surely by doing that someone could get control of Oliver and calm him down. I made it to the door and stepped out into the hallway but he was right on top of me, not letting me escape his attack. Remember it was three or four o'clock in the morning and the hallways were empty and dead quiet. That is until we stepped out of Oliver's room with swords clashing and a crowd of drunks shouting for Oliver to stop.

Clang, clang our swords echoed through the hallway. I must admit I was scared shitless for I had never been attacked by a drunken madman with a sword before (or since). I had to come up with another plan of escape before one of us really got hurt or killed. I knew that at the end of the long hallway there was a fire escape which was a circular slide that ended up on the ground floor of the hotel. I thought that if I could make it to that I would dive onto the slide and surely that would be the end of the madness. So that was my plan.

The noise of our swords meeting and the cries of the other drunks filled the hallways and magnified the din of battle. As we continued the fight toward the fire escape, we came to Bette Davis's room and the door opened. There stood Miss Davis in her nightgown (not a pretty sight). She took one look at us, screamed and quickly slammed her door.

We worked our way down the hall and passed in front of the elevator. The doors opened and there was a very elderly couple inside. When they saw two bloody fools with swords blazing, the old gentleman threw himself in front of his lady and began pushing all the buttons on the elevator panel. The door slowly closed and they were gone. We were both a mess from the sweat and blood. All of a sudden there were police with guns drawn swarming the hallways. "Halt," they ordered, "Drop the weapons." We did as ordered to my relief.

Once again I was amazed to see Oliver change from a

crazed drunken madman into a proper English gentleman. He explained that he was giving a fencing lesson to a Colonial for an upcoming motion picture. The director and producers of our film had been summoned and were frantically talking to the officer in charge. They somehow got things swept under the rug and nobody was charged with anything. Thinking back I am thankful that my agent had urged me to take sword training and learn the basics of fencing. No telling what might have happened otherwise.

Bette Davis thought I was a bit crazy and out of control after seeing Oliver and me locked in mortal combat with swords that night. I explained the whole episode was none of my doing, and that I was actually fighting for my life. I apologized for disturbing her and all seemed to be forgiven. A few weeks later the folks from *TV Guide* magazine showed up on location to shoot photos of Miss Davis for the cover. To my surprise, she grabbed me and said, "Come be in the photo with me!" So there I was on the cover of *TV Guide* with Bette Davis... How many people can brag about that? I am proud to have worked with one of Hollywood's really great actresses...Thanks Bette!

The filming moved along with more of Oliver's crazy antics. I could write an entire book on his doings but I won't for most of them were just a drug crazed alcoholic being stupid. I will relate two more short stories.

At the time we were shooting "Burnt Offerings," the film "Jaws" had just been released and was getting a lot of attention. One Friday we wrapped early so I decided to go see the film to see what all the hoopla was all about. Monday, when we resumed shooting, I mentioned to Oliver the film had scared the crap out of me, and I thought it was one of the most frightening films I had ever seen. Well of course in Oliver's eminent style, he told me I was a pussy, that he had never been scared by a movie in his life! I assured him that "Jaws" would scare him and anyone else who saw it. We argued about that until I bet him one hundred dollars that he could not see the film and not get scared.

He took me up on my bet. The next Saturday a bunch of us went to see "Jaws." The studio had called ahead and reserved the balcony for our group. We took the front row seats and settled in to watch the film. Oliver munched a large tub of popcorn and asked me if I wanted to give him his hundred bucks now or after the film ended. I told him I would wait because it was he who would owe me the hundred bucks. The film began to roll and all was quiet in the theatre. I waited until the scene where Richard Dreyfuss was diving on the sunken boat and the rotted head pops out of a window. At that moment I grabbed Oliver's leg and shouted, "Look out!"

He came out of his seat like a shot and I thought he was going to jump over the railing. Popcorn flew in all directions. As he realized he was going to live and calmed down a bit, all he could say was, "Son of a bitch, fucking Colonial." I could see he was still a bit shaken.

Being a bit of a wise-ass I asked, "Thought you never got scared by a movie?" Needless to say, I never saw my hundred!

One last story about Mr. Reed. On a bright sunny Sunday morning Oliver had been asked to do an interview with the entertainment editor of one of San Francisco's leading newspapers. It had been arranged that he and his lady would be picked up at the hotel by the editor and driven to a local high-end restaurant for brunch and the interview. Oliver asked me to join them and could Reggie ride with me.

The editor showed up with his girlfriend in a new Bentley sedan, a beautiful shiny car that had cost some serious bucks. We followed them to the restaurant and were escorted to a private outside section overhanging the bay below. The first thing Oliver did was order four bottles of the best wine and informed everyone at the table that there would be no interview until the bottles were empty. It did not take him long to empty them. We ordered and began our meal, and the interview began in a casual manner. All the while Oliver slugged down mixed drinks. Reggie whispered in my ear, "This is not going to be pretty." I knew what he meant for I to could see Ollie's eyes becoming more and more half cast and red. The poor man trying to interview him was getting nowhere and we could see the frustration in his face.

When we finished our meal the waiter brought us each a bowl of sherbet ice cream. Oliver looked at it through very bloodshot eyes and informed everyone, "This interview is over." He then stood up, picked up his bowl of sherbet and dumped it on top of his head, walked over to the railing and leaped off into the bay below. None of us could believe what he had just done. The waiter rushed to the phone and called the rescue squad while the rest of us made our way out of the restaurant to the shoreline below.

We reached the shore and saw Oliver stagger out of the surf in his beautiful English made suit. He staggered straight to the Bentley and plopped himself dripping wet and muddy on the leather back seat of the car. I thought the poor editor was going to have a heart attack as he watched the scene play out. About that time the rescue squad and police showed up. They removed Oliver from the car, put him on a gurney and examined him to see if he was injured. The editor and his lady wasted no time making an exit from the scene. Needless to say the interview never ran in the paper!

As the film drew on, the tension and lack of rest took a toll on the cast and crew. There were nights nothing was done because of special effects going bad that had to be reset and reshot, nights of just waiting for something to happen to break the monotony. I had slowly tried to get away from going to the bar every night with Ollie and the gang. It beat me up too much so I would make excuses when asked to join them. My room had a roof just below the window which allowed me to slip out my window to the parking lot below. I would go out and do my own thing then return the same way.

I had met a young lady on the set and made a date for dinner with her. Somehow Ollie got word of this and insisted that we join him and his group for drinks later that evening. Well as luck would have it, my lady friend just happened to be a real movie buff and insisted that we join them, which we did. It turned out that she was not an experienced drinker and after a few drinks became a drunken love goddess who insisted that we go back to my room. Being a young southern gentleman I could only do one thing, take her back to my room.

It was late and I informed the group we were leaving. I thanked them for a nice evening and was about to make my exit when Ollie stood up and informed me that it was rude to leave a party early and he made a big scene. We left anyway and went to my room and were enjoying some private time together when we heard Ollie and his group return. There was a knock at my door and I could hear a very drunken Ollie shouting for me to open up. The young lady was a bit shaken—she was not used to all this Hollywood craziness. I assured her that if we were quiet he would go away in a few minutes. Boy was I wrong. All of a sudden there was a crash and my door literally shattered as Ollie came crashing through with Reggie and the group right behind him. I never saw that young lady again and had a hell of a time explaining to the hotel what happened to my door.

It seemed like the film was cursed for every day things got crazier. We had some very tricky make-up effects at the end of the film where our lead actress turned into a crazy old lady possessed by the house. To create those effects involved face casts and creating rubber pieces to achieve the wanted look.

I must add here that our actress, aside from being a Looney

Tune, was pregnant for the first time and read every book she could on having a baby. Like most actresses, she would have every symptom, every ache and pain she read about, we went through protein deficiencies, irritable bowel syndromes, hot flashes, you name it—she had experienced it. It was a joke on the set. It wasn't a joke to me because I had to put up with her drastic mood swings from hour to hour, along with the fact that she was a nut case anyway, which made my job even harder.

One afternoon as I was working with her she informed me that she had to take a break because she had to pee. So we stopped what we were doing. I expected her to go next door to the rest room and do her thing. To my amazement and disbelief, she went to the coffee table took a Styrofoam cup from the table, placed it in the middle of the floor, lifted her dress, squatted over it and began to pee through her pantyhose into the cup, or should I say almost it into the cup. I could not believe my eyes. At first I was shocked, then I got mad, there are just a few things I won't stand for and I guess that was one of them. I grabbed my make-up case and left the room. I went to the director and told him what had just taken place and that I would not be working with this nut case anymore. They had to bring in someone else to work with her for the remainder of the film.

A few months after finishing the film I got a call from Oliver wanting me to do another film called "The Lion in the Desert" with him and Anthony Quinn. I made sure I was busy working on another project when the start time for that film rolled around.

A bit of irony, while shooting the film "Gladiator," Oliver Reed died in a bar. It has been said that no one there knew he had died for about fifteen minutes, they all thought he had just passed out. They say his last spoken lines, before they had to computerize his image to finish the film were, "I AM AN ACTOR!" It's fitting and I know Ollie would have loved it, for he was in deed a great actor!

THE LOST MAN

In the fall of 1969 I was at Universal Studios prepping for a feature film called "The Lost Man" starring Sidney Poitier. I was hired as the second man on the film, the department head being Marvin Westmore, one of the famous Westmores of Hollywood make-up fame. The department head is usually the make-up artist that runs the show and takes care of the stars, the second man does all of the other actors and effects on the film.

While packing and going over the supplies for the film Marvin told me he wanted to make me a deal. I had no choice being the second so I ask him what kind of deal he wanted to make. He told me that if I would take care of Mr. Poitier, he would do everybody else on the shoot. I had no choice so I agreed,

thinking to myself that he must know something about Sidney that I did not... Maybe he was a big pain in the ass!

I didn't meet Sidney before leaving for our location in Pennsylvania, so I had no clue what was in store for me until the first day, or should I say the first night, of the shoot. Our first location was on the docks of Pittsburgh, in a very rough and dangerous location. It was damp and very cold with heavy fog.

Sidney arrived on set, and I introduced myself and asked if there was anything special he wanted or needed from the make-up department. He was very professional and courteous and wanted nothing special. After doing his make-up that first night I thought to myself that he was not too bad and seemed like a nice guy. Everything went well for the first few nights of filming. I had no problems, but Sidney seemed a bit cold and standoffish, for some reason we had not clicked or entered into a friendly relationship. Most of the time a make-up artist gets to know the actor or actress pretty well and a friendship develops, but so far that had not happened with Sidney. One very cold and damp night the prop man placed fifty gallon drums in various sites and started fires in them to keep the crew warm. That night a few crew members and I had partaken a few nips of antifreeze from one of our local crew members and were feeling no pain.

Sidney finished a scene, came to the fire and began dancing about trying to warm up. I watched him for a while and being a smartass, as I am at times, very loudly exclaimed "Well look at that, they all have rhythm." You could have heard a pin drop. Everyone looked at me in disbelief. Sidney stopped and gave me a deadly stare... I tensed up and got into a defensive stance, ready to fend off his coming attack.

He slowly advanced on me and just as he was in striking distance, he broke into a big smile and said, "Yeah! And all you white guys all look the same." There was an immediate roar of laughter from the other crew members. From that point on Sidney and I became close friends; I worked on another three films with him! I must say Sidney Poitier was one of the classiest, finest actors I have had the privilege to meet and work with; he's the real deal, one of Hollywood's finest!

While filming in Philadelphia we were staying at the old Warrick Hotel, one of the city's finest old Victorian hotels. Returning to our rooms one Friday night after the first weeks shooting we were all in for a big surprise! Our rooms had been robbed, not just looted but cleaned out, everything, even our clothes were gone. Everyone was in a major panic for we were left with almost nothing. The hotel police along with the city cops showed up to investigate but got nowhere. None of the hotel employees knew or heard anything. It was as if a herd of ghosts had descended from the other side and took everything. After a few days of the cops bungling about and doing their impression of Barney Fife we knew we were in trouble and that we would most likely never see our belongings.

When we first arrived in Philadelphia, Sidney and a few of the producers had a meeting with the black gang leaders in the area where we would be filming. Each block was controlled by a different street gang and if we did not want trouble, we had to hire a different gang for security each time we moved. It was a very dangerous area to say the least. Of course, all the gang leaders knew Sidney and respected his efforts to get more black actors work in Hollywood.

Sidney knew the local police were getting nowhere finding our belongings. He announced Sunday evening that he had called for a meeting with the street gang leaders on their turf (deep in the ghettos). The producers and the cops did not want him to go into the ghetto without an escort for it was too dangerous. He informed them that he was going and that a couple of his guys were going with him, he assured them he would be okay. Later that evening he called a meeting with cast and crew. He told us that Monday, when we returned to our rooms, all our belongings would have been returned to us. As promised, almost everything was back in our rooms Monday night... Sidney had performed a miracle! We were a happy bunch, to say the least!

Another example of what a good guy Sidney Poitier is and his care for his crew and cast happened the first week of shooting. That first night when dinner break was called we all lined up at the caterers, as crews always do. We were each given a brown paper bag with a cheese sandwich, an apple and a small bag of potato chips. We all thought that was bullshit. A dinner meal, by union rules, was to be a hot sit-down dinner, not a friggin' cheese sandwich.

We all complained and were assured that tomorrow it would be different. The next day we began shooting days, and sure enough when lunch was called it was the same thing, a cheese sandwich (now I have nothing against a good cheese sandwich but these were just two pieces of old white bread a dab of mayonnaise and a thin slab of cheese). Well the next day it was the same old thing and the next. On the third day when lunch rolled around, Sidney called us all together and told us to take a two hour lunch and to go eat anywhere we wanted but bring back the receipt and production would pick up the tab. We all did and if I remember the total cost to the producers was over three thousand dollars and lost production time.

After that we had a caterer called Momma Rosas' Soul Food that was with us until filming was completed. We had some of the best food that any crew had ever had on location! Again thanks to Sidney for watching out for the people he was working with. I went on to do three other films with Sidney before retiring. It was a real pleasure working with him and I treasure the memories of those days.

A MAKE-UP ARTIST'S REVENGE

There are always shows where you have to work with one of the Hollywood kiss-asses or brown-nosers. We all know the type, no talent but friends with the director or actor, usually they want to be an actor but can't make it on his or her merit so they kiss up to someone who they think can help them…Well Hollywood is full of them! The first lesson someone in the film industry learns if you are a professional, is to treat everyone on the crew with respect. Everyone is there to do the best job they can to make a good film.

There are some that need to learn a lesson the hard way, you just have to teach them the proper respect everyone on the set deserves. It is really stupid if you are an aspiring actor, even if you are kissing the director's ass to hassle the make-up artists. I will relate a few stories here that emphasize that point.

STORY ONE

Back in the late sixties we were shooting a series called "Jericho," set in World War Two France, about the French underground fighters. It was being filmed at MGM studios on Lot Three. The shooting took place mostly at night and Lot Three at night was one cold damp location. I had fellow make-up artist, John Norin, working with me on the project. As make-up artists our work was pretty simple, keep our actors and extras dirty with an occasional blood effect or wound.

On that shoot we had a real pain-in-the-ass friend of the director working as an extra who was always in everybody's business, always sneaking around trying to find something he could report to the director., Everyone hated that little worm. As the shoot progressed John and I would take turns and sneak off behind one of the sets and get a few hours' sleep. One night the little rat found out what we were doing and reported it to the director, who in turn told the first assistant director, who came to us and gave us a bit of an ass chewing.

A few nights later God smiled on us and our little rat came rushing into the make-up area all a dither full of himself and announced, "I need a mustache for the next scene!" I tried to explain to him in a professional manner that we did not have any mustaches with us, for they were not listed on the call sheet. He went ballistic shouting and screaming that this was his big chance, the director had given him lines but he needed a mustache so he wouldn't be recognized from another shot. Again I told him we had no mustaches, that if this were a western we would always have a supply on hand, but this was a world war two film that did not require them (of course, both John and I had mustaches in our supplies). He ran back to the director and cried on his shoulder a bit and then returned to us. He was in a complete panic. "You've got to do something to help me," he pleaded.

I looked at John, gave him a wink and a bit of a smile, he rolled his eyes for he knew something was coming. "There is one thing we can do," I told the rat, "We could trim some of your hair and lay on a mustache with it, but that's up to you."

His eyes got big and he said, "Let's do it, how long will it take?"

"Just a few minutes," I replied.

"Well let's do it. They are waiting for me." As John watched, I took hold of the front locks of his hair and cut them off as close to the scalp as I could. Of course he did not realize what I had just done. I laid a nice mustache on him, placed his hat back on his head so he could not see the front of his hairline and sent him on his way. I thought John and I would bust a gut laughing as the rat scurried off to do his big scene. We could hear his screams as he discovered what I had done. For many weeks after that he wore a hat every day, but you know what? He never gave us a hard time again!

Make-up artists are a funny lot and sometimes it takes a while for the new actress or actor to realize that. A real professional actor, who has been trained, will know that the make-up people can help make or break your career. If you piss off the make-up man on the show he can make you look like homemade soap on camera just by doing the simplest thing with the shadowing or colors he uses. I know of many times that a young actor or actress has come in all full of his or herself and given the make-up person a hard time or was being a pain in the ass for no reason except for an over inflated ego. When the dailies were screened the next day, he or she came out looking like they had just come off a weekend bender.

A little advice to the new actor, come in knowing your lines, be able to hit your mark, take the director's directions and be kind to your make-up artist and crew. If you can do this you can consider yourself a professional and everyone you are working with will respect you and help you look good on film… It takes a whole crew to make a film!

DON'T MESS WITH THE MAKE-UP ARTIST!!!

Revenge can be had in many ways, and as a make-up artist it can be real sweet. Here is a little story of one of those times.

In 1965 I found myself working with David L. Wolper Productions on a television special called "Primal Man," later changed to "In Search of Man." It was dealing with early man or cavemen to some. We were shooting in the mountains up near Mammoth, California in a remote location up to our asses in snow. I had good friend and make-up artist, Wes Dawn, working with me on the project. Our job was to create cave man looking characters out of our actors which entailed laying forehead and nose appliances each morning. This process had to be done right the first time otherwise one had to start over and redo the whole process which took time, and time is always costly on a film. After the appliances were applied, we then lay a beard and shaggy wig on each actor and dirty them down to give them the look our director wanted. The normal way we did that was to use spirit gum to attach the beard and a colored hair spray, called Streaks and Tips, to give them the dirty appearance. Both of these products were easily removed at the end of the day's shooting.

As always there was the proverbial ass-kisser and friend of the producer who had no talent for anything except sucking up to anyone he thought might help him. He was like a little gnat, always in your face doing nothing but causing trouble and getting in the way. Everyone on the shoot hated the little bastard, but because of his position, had to tolerate him and his crap.

Then came our day, it was perfect, the last day of shooting and the last shot of the day. He came bursting into the make-up trailer all full of himself and announced, "I'm playing one of the cavemen in today's shot and I need to be made up right away!"

Thank you, Lord, I thought. "Have a seat," I told him and began doing a make-up job on him. Now this is absolutely true! I applied the beard, but instead of using spirit gum I used good old contact cement and I used a lot of it. Next came what should have been Streaks and Tips, but I substituted spray- on brown leather dye. When I was done I patted him on the back and sent him out to the set. Wes and I had a good laugh and quickly started packing our gear for our trip back to our room. We wanted to get out of Dodge before they called a wrap and the little prick realized what we had done.

Days later I had a phone call from our victim asking me how to remove the make-up. It seemed he could not quite get it off and he had tried everything, his face was broken out and he had pulled some of his hair out trying to remove it. I explained to him that I did not understand his difficulty for all the other actors on the show had no problem removing it.

A sad note about this shoot, the crew returning to Hollywood chartered a flight out of Mammoth Airport. Wes and I watched the plane take off and crash directly into the mountain killing everyone on board. I guess it was fate that Wes and I had met a couple of local girls and decided to stay a couple of days and do some skiing… Thank you, God!

WINCHESTER 73

In the summer of 1967 I was working at Universal Studios on the remake of "Winchester 73" starring Tom Tryon, John Saxon, Dan Duryea and Joan Blondell. This is a story about an incident that could have been tragic if it had not been for the professionalism of our cast, especially John Saxon. The scene was in the sheriff's office, we had great character actor, Paul Fix, playing the sheriff who had Saxon in jail. The action was Saxon's escape from jail… No big deal, right?

We went through several rehearsals for lighting and camera, doing the entire scene with the exception for the shot killing the sheriff. In rehearsal the prop man had placed a wooden bowl of dummy cartridges on the desk for Saxon to simulate loading the Winchester rifle he used for the scene. When it came time to shoot the scene the dummies were replaced with five blank cartridges so he could shoot and kill the sheriff during his escape. As the scene progressed, and it came time to shoot the sheriff, Saxon pulled the trigger. There was a loud boom from the blank and when the smoke cleared there was a huge hole in the side of the oak desk right next to Paul Fix. It seems that the dummy cartridges placed in the bowl were of mixed calibers and one of the smaller cartridges had lodged in the barrel of the rifle. When the blank was chambered in behind it, it became a bullet.

If it had not been for the fact that Mr. Saxon was a trained professional, and knew to never actually point a gun directly at another actor, it could have been a tragic day and Hollywood could have lost a great actor. As an actor, one is trained to always point a prop gun just to the side of another actor, never point it directly at him, the camera angle will make it look like you are on target. Safety is always the top concern when firearms are used in a scene and most of the older seasoned actors have been trained how to handle firearms safely on the set!

WINTERHAWK

I think in everyone's career there is one film that stands out as being your favorite or that holds some of your fondest memories. I guess mine would have to be a little low budget film called "Winterhawk" shot in the winter of 1972. There are many reasons for my choosing this project as my favorite and why it will always hold a warm spot in my heart.

I first got involved with "Winterhawk" when my good friend Slim Pickens gave me a call and wanted me to attend a production meeting with him. He explained that there was a film project he was involved in about the mountain men that was to be filmed in northern Montana, and he wanted me to be a part of it. That evening we met with the writer/director, Charlie Pierce, at his office in Hollywood. We all seemed to hit it off right away and began rewriting the script and exchanging ideas about the story. After weeks of meetings and numerous rewrites we agreed that we had a good story with rich characters and good action. I was asked to help in getting all the elements together such as props, costumes, weapons and everything we would need to shoot the film.

I left a few days later for Kalispell, Montana where we would be shooting most of the film. At that time I was driving a 1970 Ford Bronco and it was packed to bursting point with saddles, guns, make-up supplies and other things we would need… I must have looked like the "Grapes of Wrath" going down the road, but I made the trip in three days. As I drove into the Flathead Valley that first time and saw the beautiful Flathead Lake I knew I was in paradise and felt I had come home. I checked into the Outlaw Inn and began setting up the room in which I would be working.

The next day I met with Charlie and we devised a game plan. The stuntman on the show was Bud Davis who I had worked with a few times in the past. Bud was one tough guy and a hell of a good stuntman. We were asked to attend a few horse auctions to find a hero horse for our lead actor who would play the Indian, Winterhawk.

We found a few good looking horses but most were still green (unbroken), it would be our job to break them and get them ready to film. We played bronc riders and horse trainers for a few days and were a little beat up, but we got the job done. There was one horse that stood out from the rest. It was an Arab mix that was a great looking animal and very fast. The problem was, like most Arabs, he was not too smart and sometimes hard to handle.

We needed Indians for the film, and I was given the task of finding them. I went to Browning, Montana to the Blackfoot Reservation to start my search. Browning is not a place that welcomes white folks and one did not want to be there after dark! I put the word out that we needed young men who were good riders to work in the film. After interviewing many that applied for the parts, I choose two young brothers to be our lead braves and stuntmen on the shoot. I had them report the next day to the ranch, where we had our horses boarded, to start training in the art of horse falls. The two brothers were very tough guys and would try anything we asked them to do. Both Bud and I had a great time working with them and knew we had made the right choice; they would be an asset to the film. The Rattler brothers were as tough as they come and willing students.

After a couple of weeks gathering everything we needed and hiring help for the shoot, I started wondering where Slim was. He should have arrived. I gave him a call and he informed me that Charlie had cut his throat and hired Leif Erikson to do his part in the film. I told him that I was also going to leave because we had been a team from the start of this project and I did not like sneaky underhanded dealings. He asked me to stay and watch his saddles and guns he had lent Charlie for the film and to keep him informed as to what was going on. From that point on I did not trust or respect Charlie Pierce, but I stayed on the film because Slim had asked me to.

Our first day of shooting was one to be remembered, they had hired a group of local Indians to play a Blackfoot raiding party. They were a fierce looking lot as they rode onto the set in costume and war paint. We began setting cameras and lights to shoot the scene, and while Charlie was giving instructions to our Indians all hell broke loose. Pickup trucks loaded with Indians crashed through the fences onto our set. They bailed out and began a huge brawl with our Indian actors. It was a real nasty fight with ax handles and various other clubs and weapons used. The crew, including yours truly, all dove for cover. That was a serious bloody fight.

In a few minutes the local police, sheriffs and the Indian police descended on the scene and after a bit got the two groups separated and calmed down. The problem was that our casting people had hired a group of Flathead Indians to play Blackfoot warriors in the scene, not knowing that the Flathead and Blackfoot are bitter enemies. After a bit of negotiations the problem was solved. We would have the Flatheads work another day and the Blackfoot would get in costume and war paint and be our war party for that day's shoot. We all learned a lesson that day and would never make that mistake again. So our first day's shoot had been pretty exciting and would set the stage for things to come.

A normal day would have Charlie and the actors take off in Charlie's big fancy bus and the rest of the crew would follow him like a parade. When he found a spot he wanted to shoot a scene, Little Joe (prop man and jack-of-all-trades) would jump out and cut a fence. We would quickly set up cameras and steal the shot and get the hell out of Dodge before being caught by the land owner. It was a low budget film and Charlie did not have permits for most of the filming we did. It was fly by night productions but a lot of fun!

Our lead actor playing Winterhawk was Michael Dante who claimed that he was a good rider and would ride anything we had. Both Bud and I questioned him about riding the little Arab. We told him that he was a bit spooky and we could have a stunt double do the riding if he was not sure of his abilities. He assured us that he could handle it, so we got everything ready for his first shot in the film. It was an easy shot: Winterhawk rides across a small stream into camp and up to a tepee to dismount . . . no problem, right?

Action was called and Michael began his ride into camp. Being an actor and wanting to make a dramatic entrance, he urged the Arab into a trot to cross the stream. That was a very bad idea. The horse blew up, jumped the stream and took off for parts unknown. I told you earlier that horse was fast, very fast. Off Michael went, holding on for dear life completely out of control, we watched as he slowly disappeared over the hill. Our wranglers took out after him and finally caught up with him and his runaway horse. When they returned to base camp Michael was a wreck, shaken to the bone. After that most of the riding was done by Bud Davis or one of our wrangler girls named Claudia.

It always amazed me what actors and their egos would do to draw attention to themselves and make them feel important. Here is one example. As I told you before we were all staying at a very nice hotel called The Outlaw Inn, which had a steak house restaurant as part of the complex. At that time it was the nicest and, most expensive, joint in town. So naturally most of the cast and crew gathered there every evening which drew a lot of the locals who wanted to see a movie star.

Almost without fail our lead actor would wait to make his entrance. He would ask the receptionist to page him in about ten minutes. When the page was announced over the PA system he would stand up and look all around as if he was expecting someone, making sure he was noticed by the locals. It became a joke with everybody. One night after he had pulled that stunt, actor/friend, Denver Pyle, looked at me and said, "That damn fool makes us all look like horses' asses!"

Another example happened at a small Mexican restaurant located just behind the Outlaw Inn. It was a nice little joint with great home- made Mexican food and a nice quiet family atmosphere. We would go over there when we wanted to have a quiet meal away from the crowds at the Outlaw, plus they had great margaritas. One night a few of us were there having dinner when we heard a commotion in one of the other rooms. We went to find out what all the fuss was about. There was our lead actor, Leif Erikson, drunk as a skunk throwing a fit, crying, moaning, making an ass of himself, and sobbing that he was a big star and was not being treated with proper respect. Well the owners gave him the respect he deserved. They took him by the scruff of the neck, tossed him out the door, and told him to never come back… So much for being a big Hollywood movie star!!!

As the filming progressed the crew became one big family and every day was an adventure, we had great fun working together. It was a great feeling when a crew and cast on a film become one and all worked together towards making a good film without egos. It doesn't happen too often because Hollywood and its unions separate different departments into little groups and seldom do they come together or stray from their little clicks. Because "Winterhawk" was a low budget film some of our crew had never worked in the film industry before and were eager to learn.

After a hard week shooting we would all gather on Friday night for barbecue and to blow off steam. There was always plenty to drink and smoke. Hell, we even had two New Orleans hookers that Charlie brought down who prepared some fantastic Cajun food for us. It was a real circus and lots fun. We partied hard, ate and drank too much, then had Sunday to heal up and get ready to start all over again Monday!

My room at the Outlaw was next door to my good friend and actor, Woody Strode, who played one of our lead Indians in the film. About half way through the film his daughter, June, came to visit her dad. She was a very attractive young lady and made a hit with everyone, especially with character actor, Elisa Cook. One night we were all in the bar having a few laughs and getting ready to call it a night. All night Elisa had been drinking and hovering around June and making advances on her. Woody excused himself and told us he was off to bed; he was tired and needed to get some sleep.

I guess June was getting a bit tired of Elisa's constant advances, and she finally gave in to him. She told him to wait about an hour and come to her room. She would leave the door unlocked, and she would be in the first bedroom waiting for him. She warned him to be quiet because her dad was in the other room but was a sound sleeper—just get undressed and come to bed. Sure enough an hour later Elisa showed up, went into her darkened bedroom undressed and climbed into her bed and kissed her on the neck.

In my room next door I heard a terrible commotion, a thud in the hallway and a door slam. I went to investigate. In the hallway was poor Elisa all stunned, crumpled in a heap and trying to get to his feet. I shut the door and went back to bed. The next morning at breakfast Woody sat down with me, and I ask him what had happened last night. He told me Elisa came into his room naked and climbed into bed with him and began kissing him on the neck. Woody said, "I tossed the damn fool out into the hallway." We both had a good laugh for we knew what June had done. Elisa never made another pass at June!

About midway through shooting we had a scene where Guthrie (Leif Erikson) had to shoot a large buffalo bull. Our director wanted Guthrie to actually shoot the animal on screen. I knew I had to do something about this, I could not let this go, this was an opportunity for me, the great mountain man and buffalo killer, to actually get a chance to really shoot one. Right then and there I formulated a plan. The evening before we were to shoot the scene I joined Leif for dinner. I asked him how he felt about the scene and the fact that he had to kill the buffalo. I could see he was a bit uneasy. "I've never killed anything before," he admitted, "I'm a bit nervous about this shot."

That was my cue. I asked him how good a shot he was with a fifty caliber Hawken muzzle loading rifle. "I've never shot one before, except with a blank charge," he admitted.

I put on my best surprised and worried look, "Do you know how dangerous this scene is? Do you know what a wounded buffalo can do to a fellow?" His eyes got big. I could see I had him!

"What are you talking about?" he asked.

I laid it on him hard and some of it was true. "Well, let me tell you. If you happen to wound that animal and he does not go down with your first shot, he will likely turn on you and charge. They might look big and clumsy, but they are fast. He will be on you before you can get out of the way." I saw that I had his attention so I continued, "I have read many accounts of old buffalo hunters gored and trampled to death by wounded bulls. They are to be taken very seriously; they could easily kill you. I told him that he should go over and talk to the rancher who was supplying the animal for the shoot and get his opinion about how dangerous doing the shot really was.

The next morning he went directly to the rancher and asked him what he thought about shooting the buffalo with a black powder rifle. I had already let the rancher in on what I was doing and he went along with it one hundred per cent. He told Leif that shooting a big bull buffalo was one of the most dangerous things he had ever heard of and thought it put the actor in great danger of being badly hurt or maybe even killed. As Leif left I could see he was visibly shaken and a bit pale, my hooks were in!

"Well, what did he tell you?" I ask him.

"I guess you were right," he told me. "I don't know what to do. I'm no hunter, not even a good shot. I'm telling Charlie that I won't do that scene, they'll have to cut it out."

"Wait, I have an idea. I could double you for that scene. "We're about the same size, and I could grey my beard and hair. Hell, nobody will know."

DOUBLING LEIF ERIKSON "WINTERHAWK"

He looked at me like I was crazy, "Are you sure you want to do that?" he asked.

"I'm sure," I answered. "Heck, I have hunted all my life. I am an expert shot with a black powder rifle and have always wanted to shoot a buffalo. If you get it okayed with Charlie, I'll be glad to do it for you."

He thought that was great and went to find

Charlie to make the arrangements for me to double for him in the shot. I could see Charlie giving me the evil eye as Leif explained what we were going to do. Charlie came to me after their meeting, "That was a pretty slick move. You ran a pretty good con on Leif, but you don't fool me, all you wanted to do was to shoot that buffalo."

I assured him that was exactly what I wanted to do, but I was also doing him a big favor, to drop that animal with one shot for the scene to work. "I can do that. Leif would have most likely wounded it or missed it all together."

"So you think you can drop it with one shot?" he asked.

"I know I can and will. In fact I will wager one week's pay on it. If I miss, I will work for one week free, but if I drop him you have to purchase a full Montana big game hunting license for me."

We agreed and I dressed in Leif's buckskin outfit, grayed my hair and beard, loaded the Hawken rifle with two hundred and twenty grains of FFG black powder, seated a one hundred thirty grain lead ball on top of it and headed to my mark on the set. I noticed Charlie had taken a spot atop the motor home with Leif to watch. Charlie had a high powered scope rifle with him just in case I missed.

The rancher released the buffalo, Charlie called, "Action." I took a steady aim at the huge beast and gently squeezed the trigger, with a loud boom the Hawken roared and belched flame and clouds of black powder smoke. I knew I had a good sight on the buffalo as I pulled the trigger, but could not see where I had hit because of the smoke from the rifle. I heard a cheer from the crew so I figured I had dropped him, and as the smoke cleared I saw the great beast lying where he had fallen, killed with one shot from a Hawken rifle. I walked back to the motor home where Charlie and Leif met me and congratulated me on my good shot. I reminded Charlie about our wager and sure enough in a couple of days I had a big game hunting license in my hot little hand.

Another funny story about doubling actors happened one cold early morning. Bud asked me if I would double actor Jimmy Clem for a horse stunt we needed to shoot that morning. I agreed, because it put a few extra bucks in my pocket. Jimmy was a big old boy, tipping the scale at well over three hundred pounds, so as I put on his wardrobe they stuffed my costume with pillows until I looked like the Pillsbury doughboy. I could just barely waddle. Then they hung an eight and a half pound brass blunderbuss musket around my neck and a powder horn and shot pouch on my side. I was helped onto my horse and found they had thrown a slick deer hide over the saddle to hide the bucking strap. I was an accident waiting to happen.

With all the pillows stuffed in my costume and the slick deer skin over my saddle, I had no control of my seating in the saddle. The scene was: a Blackfoot ambush sent Jimmy on his run-away horse right into another war party. Jimmy was thrown from his horse and taken prisoner. It was a pretty easy

DOUBLING JIMMY CLEM WINTERHAWK

stunt under ordinary conditions, but with all my padding and not being able to get a good seat in the saddle, when I pulled the bucking strap to start the horse bucking. I was launched like a missile leaving the launching pad. I remember the first flip then everything went black for a few minutes. As I came to my senses I was surrounded by fierce looking Indians poking and jabbing me with tomahawks and spears. Charlie called, "Cut." He came over and said we needed to do another take, then broke into a big grin . . . needless to say we got it in one take!

Normally that late in December the Flathead Valley would be covered in snow, but that year was different—we had not a flake of the white stuff. We were at the point in the story where we needed snow to continue shooting. Each day we would check the forecast hoping for a storm or at least a little flurry so we could film. After a few days sitting around the bar at the Outlaw twiddling our thumbs, Charlie decided we had to shoot something, but how without snow?

I remembered something an old special effects man had told me about shooting silent films in the early days of Hollywood. I told one of our local drivers to go out and buy as much Tide laundry soap as he could find and report back to the make-up room at hotel. I know he thought I was crazy, but we were paying him to run errands and pick up supplies so off he went. I told Charlie what my idea was and he agreed to give it a try. That afternoon we took two of our actors, Dennis Fimple and L.Q. Jones, out to a sight on a mountainside for a scene where Dennis kills L.Q. I gave boxes of Tide to several members of the crew and told them to start spreading it around behind our actors and in the trees if they could get it to stick. It worked great, on film it looked exactly like snow.

If you see the movie "Winterhawk," look for the scene where L.Q. Jones is killed. Notice the background, it's all soap! Today that hillside is the cleanest in the Flathead Valley. That little trick worked for that shot, but we still needed snow. The days went by with no snow and no forecast of any storms on the horizon.

We were at the point we had to have snow to continue filming, it was dead time for us with nothing to do but hang around the Outlaw and kill time. We did everything we could come up with to pass the time, we always seemed to end up in the bar hoping someone would come up with something exciting to do. One day Woody and a few of us were telling war stories about films we had worked on and Woody brought up "The Professionals." I asked him about the bow and arrows he had used in the film. A big smile came on his face, "I have it in my room. I'll get it and we can take it outside and shoot it."

He left, and in a few minutes returned with the bow and a quiver full of arrows. Wow! This is great, I thought having done some shooting with a bow a few years back. Woody took an arrow from the quiver, notched it in the bow and handed it to me, "Let's see if you can hit that large knot in the ceiling." (The Outlaw Inn has beautiful knotty pine ceilings.) I thought he was kidding and handed the bow back to him. He drew the arrow back and let it fly, embedding the arrow deeply into the ceiling right next to the knot. Then he handed me the bow. Well what could a fellow do except take the shot, which I did, my arrow hit right next to Woody's.

About that time the owner came bursting into the room raising all kinds of hell about shooting arrows into his ceiling. Woody calmed him down and told him that those two arrows would lead to a lot of stories about when Hollywood stayed at the Outlaw Inn. To this day I think the two arrows are still there.

Out of desperation snow making machines were brought from New York to try to get the snow we needed. They ran for over a week and did not make one flake of the white stuff. Production made a decision. The only place they could find the snow we needed was in the small town of Purgatory, Colorado which was nearly four hundred miles away. The next morning we were off to Purgatory.

We must have looked like a traveling circus as we motorcade across the country. Charlie's big fancy motor home led the pack followed by prop trucks, two large trucks hauling horses, wardrobe vans, lighting and grip trucks and various personal vehicles. If I remember there were fourteen vehicles in our entourage. We finally arrived in Purgatory and settled in our living quarters which were great.

We stayed at one of the local ski resorts which had not yet opened for the season. We had beautiful cabins or condos all to ourselves which were very upscale and luxurious, all this and no women …What a waste! We were the only people on the mountain except for the ski patrol who were preparing the slopes for the coming ski season.

We would shoot about five hours each day and then call a wrap because of the cold. We went back to our rooms, cleaned up and headed into Steamboat Springs for dinner and a few drinks—that is if we could get off the mountain. I had to leave the shoot a week before filming ended because I had to start a pilot for a new television show called "Nakia" starring Robert Forrester.

As promised, I gave Slim Pickens a call and told him that I was leaving the shoot that next day. He asked me to pick up all of his saddles and guns from props and bring them home with me, which I did. I know Slim was very hurt by what Charlie had pulled on him after all the work he had put into that film project. I think Charlie paid the price in the long run for "Winterhawk" would have been a much better film if Slim had played the Guthrie part that Leif ended up playing. After all, Slim was the real thing. Leif was just another Hollywood actor playing a part. I cannot complain too much for I got to work with and know some of the greatest character actors in the business. Some would become lifelong friends, folks like Denver Pyle, L.Q. Jones, Dennis Fimple, Woody Strode, Arthur Honeycutt, and Elisa Cook. As I said before "Winterhawk" will always hold a warm spot in my heart.

OH SHIT, NOT THIS OLD BOY!

I was, and probably will always be, a country boy, but in my early days working in Hollywood I was very naive to the ways of the big world.

I had a call from a buddy of mine, Leo Gordon, who you will know as one of Hollywood's greatest character actors and heavies (bad guys). What you most likely don't know is Leo was also a very good script writer. He called to ask me if I wanted to work on a World War Two film he had written called, "Tobruk," about the German Africa Corp  fighting in the desert. Well, being an avid history buff of that era and a collector of WWII memorabilia, I jumped at the chance. The film was shot at Universal Studios and on location in the desert near Palm Springs.

My first day on the film I had my offices and make-up room set up in the head make-up department at the studio. That morning Bud Westmore, the head of Universal Studios' make-up department, came into my room and asked me if I would mind doing him a favor and do actor Rock Hudson's make-up for a few days until his regular make-up man returned. Of course I agreed. A bit later Mr. Hudson showed up, introduced himself and I began doing his make-up. He seemed to be a very nice guy and we hit it off right away. As he left my room that first morning I was pretty excited and a bit full of myself. I had just made up one of Hollywood top stars and he seemed to like me…I was a big shot!

Everything that first day went smoothly. We were busy keeping our actors and extras dirty and applying blood effects where they were needed. The next morning Mr. Hudson arrived early for wardrobe and make-up and was in a really good mood, telling jokes and stories of some the funny things that had happened in his early days in the business. I really took a liking to him. He was very considerate of the crew and seemed like one of the guys, there was nothing Hollywood about him. At lunch that day I did something which I never do, I asked him if I would sign a photograph for me, he said sure that he would bring me one the next morning.

Sure enough the next morning when he arrived for make-up he gave me a brown manila envelope, "Here's the picture you asked for," he said as he handed it to me. I thanked him but did not open the envelope. I had a lot of bullet wounds and blood effects I had to get done that morning and had no time. When I reported to the set that morning he asked me how I liked the photo. I thanked him again and told him that it was great and how much I appreciated it. Of course I had not opened the envelope he had given me for I had no time; it was still back in my room where I had left it.

That evening when I returned to the studio to get everything ready for the next day's filming I opened the envelope … Oh my God, was I surprised and shocked … In my hand was a 8x10 glossy photo of Mr. Hudson reclining on a love seat, naked as a jay bird with everything standing at attention, signed "For Al, Love Rock." I thought to myself this has to be a joke, then I remembered telling him how I loved the photo. At first I didn't know what to do. As I said, I was in shock, and then I began to get angry. I knew I could not face him again for fear that I might lose it and smack him. I made a beeline for Bud Westmore's office and told him of my dilemma and embarrassment. "I thought everyone knew about Rock," he answered. Everyone except me! I thought to myself.

That was my last day on "Tobruk." I went to my room and shredded the photo, which thinking back was stupid because that photo would be worth quite a bit today. But Hommie don't play those games and it had my name on it.

NOBODY LIKES FLAPPING EAGLE

Now there's a catchy title that will draw lots of folks into a movie theatre. Well that's what I was working on back in November of 1970. It had all the elements to be a good film, directed by Carol Reed, starring Anthony Quinn, Claude Akins and Shelley Winters. It was a comedy about the adventures of a drunken Indian played by Quinn. It was later retitled "Flap," another winner of a title. I had been working on this film for about a week when Miss Winters showed up for her first day of shooting. I had never met her but had heard all of the rumors about her appetite for younger men and had been getting a lot of ribbing from Mr. Quinn about what she would do to me when we met.

I was young, a bit shy and self-conscious so all this ribbing got to me. I will never forget that morning, it was cold and damp on the back lot of Warner Brothers Studio as I headed for Miss Winters' bungalow to do her make-up that first day. I arrived at the front door and knocked. There was no answer so I knocked again. "For Christ's sake, come on it, it's unlocked."

I sheepishly entered carrying a make-up case in each hand. "I'm here to do your make-up," I shouted as I entered.

"I'm in the back dressing room, come on back," was her reply. I entered the dressing room and was presented with a picture I'll never forget, and it was not a pretty picture. There sat Miss Winters before a large full length mirror wearing nothing but a smile. I was shocked and quickly stepped out of the room excusing myself for bursting in on her before she was ready. Needless to say, I was very embarrassed and knew that this was not the way to start the first day working with someone. She laughed and called me back into the room, "I always get my make-up done before I get dressed. You'll get used to it; after all, it can be fun!"

I told her I was uneasy with that and would appreciate her putting on a robe or something while I did her make-up. I think I even made up some lame excuse about it being studio policy. She would have nothing to do with that. She got up, came over to me put her hand on my shoulder and gave me a look that I guess was meant to be sexy. "What's your name young man?" she asked as she reached down and grabbed my crotch.

That was it. I made a quick retreat for the door with her following and screaming at me that I was not a man and demanding that I come back and do her make-up. I was out of there, I was having none of that. Don't get me wrong, I love women, and at that time in my life was pretty much a horny toad and trying to catch up with as many as I could, but Miss Winters would not be one of them. There's just something about an overweight, wrinkly, fifty-plus years old woman that just didn't appeal to me. I quit the show that morning.

It was the joke around the studio for a while and I became a legend at the Warner Brothers' lot… Oh God the price of fame! The only other run in I had with Miss Winters was years later while working on a film called "The Mad Room" with my good friend, Stella Stevens. We were working in Pasadena, California, and had very early calls each day. During that time Robert Kennedy was assassinated, and production did not want the news the get to Miss Winters for she was a big supporter of his. Well as luck would have it, that morning as we were driven to the location we passed a news stand and there in big bold print was the headline "Robert Kennedy Assassinated." She saw it and began screaming, jumped from the limo and ran down the middle of the street tearing her clothes off. The driver was right behind her. He finally caught up with her, put his jacket around her and brought her back to the car. We did not film that day.

This is another story about Robert Kennedy unrelated to the above.

I was taking an evening photo journalism course at Valley College. For my final project I chose to do a political photo story about Kennedy's campaign in Southern California. I attended every speech and rally he did in California and racked up rolls and rolls of film on him. I had press passes and was all set to attend his speech at the Roosevelt Hotel that fateful night, but at the last moment I had a call from a friend of mine asking me to shoot an album cover for weird singer, Tiny Tim. Of course I headed for Tim's place to shoot the cover for it was a paying job and I wanted to meet him to see if he was as odd in person as he was on stage. HE WAS! If I had not chosen to do the Tiny Tim job, I would have been right there on stage with Kennedy that night.

I went through all of the photographs I had taken of Kennedy, picked out six I thought were my best and sent them to Ethel, his wife, with a note about them and to express my sorrow at her loss. I was amazed to receive a letter from her a few weeks later thanking me for my thoughtfulness. It had a black border around it and the envelope had no stamp, just her signature which had been canceled just like a stamp. She had included a small metal name plate from his desk with the letter. I thought it was real class that she would take time in her hours of sorrow to write me such a letter. It is now framed and hangs on the wall in my office.

October 3, 1968

Dear Mr. Fleming,

How very kind and thoughtful of
you to write and to enclose such a
marvelous photograph of my husband.

The children and I are so grateful to you for remembering us and we
are consoled knowing you share our
sorrow.

With warm wishes

from

Ethel Kennedy

Mr. Al Fleming
14211 Moorpark
Sherman Oaks
California

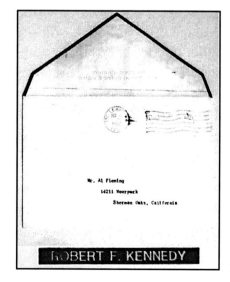

109

THE LAS VEGAS SHOW

My first really big break as a make-up artist came in 1964 when I was asked to run a stage and television show called "The Las Vegas Show," starring comedian Bill Dana. Thinking back, the only reason they asked me was that nobody else wanted to do it. The show was competition to the late night variety shows of Jack Parr and others. We would do the show at the old Hacienda Hotel and Casino, one of Las Vegas' great old original casinos. In theory it was a good idea for we had all the talent in Las Vegas at our disposal. The only problem was our host Bill Dana. His only claim to fame was the character he created for his comedy act called Jose Jimenez, the Mexican astronaut. After that he was dead in the water. The only hope for the show was the fact that we had other talented people also working on it, newcomers like JoAnne Worley, Peter Barbutti and others.

It was a hard show to do and we put in lots of hours. Our schedule was: first rehearsal at 11:00 a.m., a dress rehearsal at 2:00 p.m., and shoot the live show at 6:00 p.m. The timing was very important. It was a live show and everything had to run on time, so we had to have our act together, otherwise it screwed everything up. I had a make-up room set up just behind the stage. It was a small room but adequate for my work and close to the action just in case anything was needed.

There was a small hallway in front on my room leading to the main stage that during the tapings was like the freeway at rush hour. I had to get our guest stars in make-up and out to the stage as fast as I could and had no time to waste so I was like a factory painting cars… I was fast, but good!

One particularly busy night I was swamped for we had a number of groups appearing on the show that night and doing their make-up took longer than I had expected. I was trying to move at lightning speed to get everyone done and on the stage on time. It never fails that when you are in a hurry everything takes longer, and that was one of those nights. We had some pretty important guest stars that evening, John Wayne, The Kingston Trio, Red Foxx and Moms Mabley, and everybody wanted to meet and talk to them. Of course they chose the make-up room to do it in. I constantly asked people to leave the room so I could work and pushed and shoved them out of my way. It was a nightmare for me.

There was one shabby fellow in particular who always seemed to be right in the middle of all the folks, and every time I asked him to leave he would show up again. At one point I had reached my limit on patience and took him by the shoulder and escorted him out of my room and pushed him into the hallway to emphasize my point. "I'm too busy. Stay out of the make-up room. I can't work around you! I told him.

Finally I had everyone made-up and we started filming that night's show. All went well, but I was bushed from all the tension I was under trying to get everyone done in time. I must say that the show that night was one of the best of the series. It was the last time the Kingston Trio preformed as a group until their comeback many years later. At the end of their last number they laid their instruments on the stage and walked away. I felt a bit sad for I had always liked them and grew up listening to their music. I screwed up though. I did not realize I could have had one of the guitars or banjo's they left on the stage that night—they just left them for anyone to take. As soon as the audience and some of the stage hands realized that, there was a mad rush to get them.

When I returned to my make-up room that night to get it ready for the next day's show, the stage manager came up to me with a big smile on his face. "So you threw Howard Hughes out of your room?" he asked.

I thought he was kidding so laughed it off as a joke.

"I'm not kidding. You really did throw him out!"

I asked him what he was talking about.

"Didn't you throw someone out of your room earlier tonight?" he asked.

"Sure I asked lots of people to leave the room. I could not do my work with everybody crowding around."

"Did you actually escort someone out into the hallway and tell him to never come back?"

Then I remembered, "Well there was some old bum looking guy that was always in the way. I did ask him to leave a couple of times then escorted him out into the hallway."

"Well that was Howard Hughes you threw out. He owns this casino and half of the town."

Oh my God, I thought, *I am going to be fired for sure!*

"Don't worry. He thought it was funny and knew you had work to do. We had a good laugh about it."

I would never have guessed that the man I escorted out of my make-up room that night was Howard Hughes. He looked like a street bum, was unshaven and shabbily dressed and unkempt. Hell, if I had known, I would have offered to give him a shave and haircut, maybe he would have mentioned me in his will!

The show ran for a few weeks but we all knew that it was dead in the water; our host just could not hold the audience and show together. One morning I reported to the stage for our morning rehearsal to find all the doors had been chained shut and were being guarded by hotel security personnel. I asked what had happened and was told that the show had folded; leaving the hotel with large unpaid bills so they had locked down everything until the debts were paid. I told the guard that I had all of my personal equipment and gear inside and needed to get it out and return to Hollywood if the show was over. I was told that nothing could be removed till all the debts were cleared. I was in a very bad position for I had to get my gear out of there or I was dead in the water without it. I had a few hundred dollars in my pocket and nothing coming in, I had to get back and find a job.

I made a few calls to other crew members and to the hotel to see if I could work something out. It was no use. They wouldn't budge until the bills had been paid or the courts had made a decision about the outstanding debt. I was at a loss and in a bit of a panic about the situation, then remembered something. I had been dating Wanda, one of the showgirls, who had lived in Las Vegas all her life. On one of our first dates she took me to a small Italian restaurant across from the hotel and introduced me to a few of the guys who ran it. That became one of our main hangouts while working on the show—the food was great and I became pretty good friends with the owners. One night, we were having a drink with one of the guys and in conversation told me that if I ever had a problem while in Las Vegas to give him a call. At the time I thought nothing of it, but remembered Wanda telling me that these guys were connected and could make things happen.

I thought, *I have nothing to lose.* I went across street to talk to them. I told them the situation I was in and all the calls I had made trying to get it resolved, and asked them if there was anything they could do to help. I was told to go back to the hotel; everything would be taken care of.

Sure enough when I returned, the guard at the door greeted me like a long lost brother, unchained the door and told me I could take whatever I wanted from the stage. I told him that

I only wanted my personal gear and equipment and would get it and get out. He told me that I could have anything I wanted, to just help myself. Well, being the honest sort I only took my stuff and was off to Hollywood. To this day I am not sure what the Italian boys did, but they got things moving in a big hurry. I sent them a thank you card a few days later.

HOW THE WEST WAS WON

The story of "How the West Was Won" and the legend of Pooper Puffer will always have a special place in my heart. The year 1977 started well for me. I had a call from good friend, Burt Kennedy, who was to direct a pilot for a new western series called "How the West Was Won" loosely based on the old cinemascope film. He wanted me to meet him at MGM Studios to discuss the film. At our meeting he explained that he wanted me to do the make-up on the film and, knowing I been a student of western history, wanted me to do some research and sketches of the various Indian tribes we depicted in the film.

For the next three weeks I worked in my office at Metro and drew sketches of costumes and other items to be used by our Indians in the film. It was one of the easiest jobs I have ever had. I knew Burt hired me to do that to put a few extra bucks in my pocket, and I think he may have wanted the small watercolor sketches of Indians.

We were then off to Kanab, Utah to start shooting the film. We had a great cast: James Arness, Bruce Boxleitner, Eva Marie Saint as our leads, plus the fact that Burt Kennedy was our director, it was a win-win situation. We all knew working with Burt was always a pleasant experience for he was the nicest, kindest man you would ever work for, and I was happy to be there!

The first couple of days were spent setting up shop and hiring locals to work with us on the project. I was asked to go to the reservation with one of the locals and pick out a number of fierce looking Indians to play our war party in the film. When we arrived there was quite a crowd gathered for the casting call, all wanting to work in the film. I called for their attention and explained that we needed horsemen who were good riders and could ride bareback to play a war party. I had a show of hands and nearly all of them raised their hands. *This was great,* I thought. *Burt will have a good bunch to choose from at tomorrow's casting call.*

I told the group to come to town the next morning and the director would do the final casting there. The next morning it looked like every Indian that lived in Utah was in little town of Kanab, some in full costume, some drunk as skunks. It was a mob scene. Burt, our cameraman, and I climbed up on the flatbed of a truck and began the job of picking our fiercest looking warriors. First we asked everyone who was a good rider to raise their hands, almost everyone did. Then we asked those who were good bareback riders to raise their hands, sure enough almost all did. At this point Burt started looking at faces, wanting to pick the fiercest looking ones out of the crowd. He chose about twenty and dismissed the others telling them we would use them later on in film. He again emphasized that we needed only really good riders because we did not want anyone to get hurt, he chose nine from this last group. We took our nine warriors aside and again explained that they would be riding bareback carrying weapons and needed to be good riders, not a one of them left. We had our fierce group of warriors that would be playing a very important part in the film.

We started filming the next day. Our first shot was with Jim Arness and one of Hollywood's great character actors, Jack Elam. It was a simple shot where Jim and Jack were captured by a group of warriors. We set up for the first shot and had our war party atop a gently sloping hill. They were to ride down the hill, surround our heroes and take them prisoners. No big deal right? An easy, nothing shot.

Burt called for action, Jim and Jack started their slow ride into the shot, he then cued the Indians to start their ride down the slope. They came charging and hollering, sounding very fierce. By the time they got to our heroes, only about a third of them were still mounted on their horses, the rest were strung out down the hillside where they had fallen. It seemed like many of the expert horsemen were not quite the riders they had claimed to be. Watching that scene unfold, Jim and Jack, along with most of the crew, went into hysterics. It was a funny sight to see fiercely painted warriors charging down a slope, that one could hardly call a hill, and going ass over tea kettle off their horses.

The cut was called and the shot reset, again Burt called action and the same thing happened, not many of the Indians made it to the bottom of the hill. It got to be such a comedy that when Burt called for the Indians to attack, Jim and Jack could not keep straight faces. Finally out of desperation, Burt told the warriors to just walk the horses into the shot, capture our heroes and be done with it. After another five or six takes we were finally able to get the shot done and move ahead.

I had another make-up artist, Kenny Winsivick, working as my assistant on that film. He was a very talented young artist and a bit of a free spirit, which was why I liked him and we got along. We had a good time on the film and were shooting in one of the most beautiful parts of Utah. Our weather was great and we had a great cast and crew to work with.

At that time Kenny and I liked to smoke a little weed to take the edge off, we would take turns watching the set while the other would take long hikes into the hills looking for Indian artifacts. We had both made friends with the young getting-his-first-break actor Bruce Boxleitner. One evening he asked us if he could join us for a smoke before we went out to dinner. He did. We all hit it off really well and had some good laughs that night and ate too much (munchies, to you smokers). That became our routine after shooting ended each day. We would get cleaned up, light up in my room and have a few hits and then go out to dinner.

That went on for a few weeks. Bruce smoked our weed and never brought anything to share with us. Kenny and I thought, that wasn't right, he was an actor who made more money than us but never offered to buy any weed. Just mooched off us. I formulated a plan. The next day I picked up a very dry pile of horse droppings from the set, and rolled a nice fat joint with it. I rolled two real joints for Kenny and me. When Bruce came to the room that night I told him that I had just gotten a new batch of weed and had rolled a joint for each of us. I gave a real joint to Kenny and made sure Bruce got the horseshit. We all lit up and began enjoying our smoke.

It was hard for Kenny and me to keep a straight face as we watched Bruce greedily inhale his shit. I asked him how he liked his number. He smiled and said that he was really getting loaded. I asked, "Good Shit huh?" He smiled and agreed that it was indeed good shit. Then I told him that he was in reality smoking shit, not good shit but horseshit. Of course he did not believe me until I opened the drawer and showed him what was left of the horse pie that I had rolled his joint with.

Right then and there the legend of the Pooper Puffer was born. We had a tee-shirt made for him. The front was a steaming pile of horseshit with fly's swarming around it, above the pile was emblazed the name "Pooper Puffer." I must say Bruce was a good sport about the whole thing and we became good friends and have had some good laughs about it over the years. I think Bruce enjoys his earned Indian name, Pooper Puffer, to this day.

WHERE ANGELS GO
TROUBLE FOLLOWS

I think everyone in the film industry remembers their first big location job. Mine was in the summer of 1968 on a little film called "Where Angels Go Trouble Follows." I was working for Columbia Studios on location in Pennsylvania on a comedy film about a group of Catholic school girls and a rebellious Sister going across country on a field trip. The great thing about working on this project was the fact that I got to meet and work with some of Hollywood's greats, people I had grown up watching on the silver screen and on TV, like Rosalind Russell, Van Johnson, Milton Berle, Arthur Godfry, Robert Taylor, Binnie Barnes, Susan Saint James and Stella Stevens. Another bonus was that most of our cast was young Hollywood actresses on their first big job, and I, being a young lad in my prime, with an eye for the pretty ladies loved every minute and fell in love a number of times.

We were shooting in a beautiful little town called Ambler. You know the place, it's right next to the Amish towns of Intercourse and Bird In Hand and had great food and were very clean but not much more. Our filming went well. Everyone was great to work with and I got to know most of our cast and heard some wonderful stories about the good old days in Hollywood. Thanksgiving Day was fast approaching and our local crews had the weekend off, and some of our actors had places they had to be for the holiday. The production manager asked me if I had any plans, which I didn't. He asked me if I would take some of our actresses to see New York City. The studio would pay all our expenses and make all the arrangements. So that Friday night after we wrapped our shooting for the weekend, a group of us got on the train and went to New York City.

Now you must remember I was a country boy, I knew as much about New York City as I did about the moon, but we were on our way! On the train we decided we wanted to see the Empire State Building first, then we wanted to go shopping in The Village. In 1968 the hippie movement was going strong and most of our young actresses were about half hippie, and I must admit I was also. We had heard stories about the famous Village with its hippie and art culture and many off beat shops. It sounded like a place we needed to see. We arrived in New York about ten in the morning, decided to get something to eat, and proceeded directly to the village without checking into our hotel (The Waldorf Astoria).

There was a misty rain that morning but it did not deter us from our adventure. We were going to see and experience The Village come hell or high water. The Village was a strange place to say the least with a mixture of Hippies, artists and drug dealers all thrown into a swirling mass of humanity. We had not been there a few minutes when we were approached by someone who wanted us buy some of his weed, and of course not wanting to be rude, we did. That was a big mistake for afterwards we all went on a wild shopping spree, buying everything from tie dyed shirts to headbands. As the day progressed into early evening we were soaking wet, very stoned, and we needed to get some rest. We took a cab back to our hotel.

When we arrived at the Waldorf, we were met by the head doorman and told that we could not enter the hotel. I explained that Columbia Studios had made our reservations and that we were guests of the hotel but had not yet checked in. We were pretty much thrown out before we had set foot in the place. I guess the sight of a group of dripping wet, stoned hippies was not the clientele they wanted in their upscale snobby hotel. We returned to the train terminal and took the next train back to Pennsylvania.

When I arrived on the set Monday morning, I was met by Stella Stevens' secretary, Jane, who told me that Stella wanted to see me in her dressing room. At our meeting Stella asked me to be her make-up artist for the rest of the show, which I was more than happy to do, but there was a problem. Her regular make-up man, who was running the show, was the son of Ben Lane, the head of the make-up department at Columbia Studios. It was a very awkward situation for me, a new make-up artist on his first location job now asked to take over the make-up for one of the film's stars from the son of the head of Columbia Studios make-up department. I explained that to Stella and she assured me that she had worked the whole thing out and everything was cool. That started a lifelong friendship with Stella. We went on to do many films together and spent a lot of personal times just having fun and raising hell… She is a great lady and a hell of a good actress, I cherish the times and adventures we shared together.

SLAUGHTERHOUSE ROCK

I think almost every make-up artist at one time or another, has wanted to play a monster in a film. Well my big chance came in 1988 on a film called "Slaughterhouse Rock" that was being produced by Arista Films. I was originally hired to design and create the monster for the film as well as all the special effects. At one of our production meetings Lou George, the producer on the project, knew that I had done some acting and asked if I would consider playing the commandant and monster in the film.

I thought that would be great fun so agreed to do it. I was to design, build and play the monster. That was something I had always wanted to do since childhood watching all the classic monster films from the 1940/50s.

After weeks of designing and redesigning the monster, I got final approval on what the creature would look like and went into the process of sculpting and casting the final product. It was cool. It had all the features you would expect a scary monster to have, a big head, fangs, alien eyes, large arms and hands with very large sharp claws, the whole nine yards. I could not wait to get into the costume and make-up the first day the monster was in the film. I was going to the scare the hell out of everyone!

It took me about three hours to get into make-up and

wardrobe, and when I stepped out of the make-up room, I was the monster. Everyone on the set oohed and aahed and told me what a good job I had done creating the look of the monster. Our first shot went well; I terrorized some folks in the sewer and then sat and waited for the next shot to be lit and ready to shoot. As luck would have it, they called for the lunch break. It was at that point I realized what I had gotten myself into. I sat there with contact lenses over my eyes, large rubber arms and hands with long sharp claws and a mouth full of snap in fangs and teeth. I could not get out of make-up because it would take too long to redo it for the next shot.

So I sat looking fierce, but starving while everyone ate a hardy lunch. They did bring me some juice which I drank through a straw. Later the real problem raised its ugly head, after drinking all the juice, I had to pee, badly. I headed for the rest room then realized that I could not even undo my costume to bring the little fellow out to do his business. *What to do?* I thought. *I'm not calling for someone to help. After all I still have my dignity, and you don't know about these Hollywood types.* I managed with my clawed hand

to get the costume opened enough, and carefully brought the little fellow out to do my business even though I was not a very good shot.

That experience convinced me I never wanted to play a monster again! Each day after that was an ordeal. My face was raw from gluing and removing the appliances, and most of the time my costume was wet and smelled bad. I remember sitting in my chair unable to eat or drink. I could not scratch an itch or hear too well. My contact lenses had to be rotated before every scene to make sure they were lined up. I was a happy camper when we wrapped the film. The monster make-up and costume still stands in a corner of my studio as a reminder that if my agent calls me to audition for another monster film to say no!

So when you watch one of many horror films produced today, know that poor actor wearing all of the make-up is earning his pay check.

THEY CALLED HIM SLIM

Imet Slim Pickens in the 1950s when I was still doing the southern rodeo circuits. In those days I still lived on my father's ranch raising quarter horses and in the summers working with Brahma bulls on the Mitchell brothers' ranch, I was a cowboy and loved it. I guess the real reason I first got involved in the rodeo life was that in those days and in my crowd, the only way to get girls was to be a rodeo cowboy. So that's what I did. At first I was only involved in calf roping and a little bull dogging and some quarter horse events. I did pretty well for a sixteen year old kid and was a bit full of myself, but there was a hitch—all the girls I liked went for the bull riders. Now at that time I stood a bit over six foot four inches tall, much too tall to be a bull rider, but I thought I would give it a try anyway. One afternoon after being kidded that "you ain't shit unless you can ride a bull," I signed up to ride in the next event … Big mistake!

My big moment came, and I climbed onto the back of one of the meanest Brahma bulls God ever made in fact he wasn't much of a bull, but in my mind he was a monster. I gave the signal that I was ready, and the gate opened, and that is all I remember. I woke up in the first aid station recovery room and the first thing I saw was a silly looking clown all dressed in a matador's costume that was way too small for him with a big grin on his face. He looked down at me and said, "Son who ever told you that you are a bull rider? You ain't. They lied to you, and if I ever see you on one of those critters again I'm going to let him stomp a hole in you." He slapped me on the shoulder and was gone.

That's how I first met Slim Pickens and in those days he was actually Slim. A few days later he showed up at our ranch and bought an Army mule from my father. We had a few good laughs about my career as a bull rider and I assured him that I had not been on a bull since. That started a lifelong friendship with one of Hollywood's great character actors and one of the nicest people you could ever meet. Slim was just one of those rare people who come into your life and make a difference. He was the real deal, down to earth, honest and not a drop of phony blood in him. I was very lucky and proud to call him a friend.

We lost contact for a few years while I lived in Florida, but as soon as I made it to California, I looked him up. I remember one of the first places he took me was to Fat Jones' Livestock Ranch in the San Fernando Valley. At that time Jones supplied most of the horses and rolling stock for the studios. It was a magical place for a young kid from Florida. There were stage coaches, covered wagons, even chariots used in the film Ben Hur, and the characters there were like the Who's Who of the stunt and Hollywood world. We spent the day hanging around with folks like Ben Johnson,

Yakima Canutt, Joel McCrea, and Jock Mahoney, listening to great tales of films they had done and funny things that had happened while they worked on them. I wish I had had a tape recorder to preserve them for all to hear.

I told Slim that I was thinking of quitting my job and seeing if I could make it on my own there in Hollywood. He asked me what I planned to do. I told him that I had an offer to work for Arvo Ojala, teaching fast draw and working in his leather shop, and wanted to give it a try. At that time Arvo had invented the modern fast draw holster and was making a name for himself teaching many of the big stars how to draw and shoot a single action Colt revolver. I had saved for months and bought one of his holsters and a Great Western single action revolver and became the fast draw terror of all the bull frogs living in my Florida neighborhood. Slim's advice was to give it a try and if I needed anything to let him know.

As everyone knows Slim was a big outdoors man. He loved hunting, fishing and just being in the high lonesome, so was asked by many manufacturers of outdoor equipment to be the spokesman for their products. I got a call from Slim one morning asking if I wanted to go to Las Vegas with him to attend the S.H.O.T. Show. Of course I said yes. The S.H.O.T. Show is an annual event where the manufacturers of outdoor equipment come to show and take orders for their new products for the coming year; it is a pretty big event and attended by thousands.

On our four-hour drive to Vegas we talked about old times, history and told jokes all the way. Slim told me he had seen one of my small parts on the television series "Laramie" and thought I had done a good job. He asked me if I was going to pursue acting as a career. I told him that I was thinking about that but had not made up my mind yet. He gave me some good advice that I have never forgotten. Before you jump into something, watch what happens when I arrive at the show and see if this is something you want for the rest of your life.

We arrived at the show and we were greeted by its promoters and VPs from some products who wanted Slim to endorse their goods. Soon a crowd had gathered around him. He told me that I should go ahead and look around; he would be there for a bit. I spent the next few hours looking at all the new toys offered by vendors. When I returned to where I had left Slim, he was still there with even a bigger crowd around him. That night at dinner he looked at me very seriously and asked, "Is that what you want?" I knew what he was asking me and without much thought I told him no.

Fame is a funny thing; everyone knows you and wants to be your friend. They want your autograph and photos with you. They love you, but without meaning to, they steal your life away. I saw that with Elvis and now with Slim. There is nowhere you can go that people don't recognize you and feel they know you because they see you all the time on television or in films.

I felt sorry for Slim because there was nowhere he could go that his fans didn't crowd him. He had very little privacy, and I think that is one of the reasons he liked being in the mountains away from folks.

That taught me a lesson. At one time I thought it would be cool to be famous and have people recognize you and want to be around you, but the price one has to pay is too high. I never wanted to be a star after that.

In 1974 Warner Brothers started making a film called "Blazing Saddles," a comedy western directed by Mel Brooks. At that time Slim lived in Columbia, California, quite a drive from Hollywood, so he would bunk with me during the week and go home on the weekends. Every night when he came home from filming he filled me in on what had happened on the set that day. He told me there was no way the film would ever be shown, it was too off color, funny but off color.

"Damn," he said, "They call people niggers and make all kinds of racial jokes that the studio will never let slip by." After hearing so many things that happened while filming, I agreed with him that this film would never fly... Boy, were we wrong. It was a big hit for Warner Brothers and Mel Brooks and quite tame by today's standards!

As everybody knows, Slim was a legendary eater, he really loved food. One Sunday morning he called and asked me if I knew anyone who liked elk steaks. He had twelve marinating ready to cook, but none of his family liked them. I assured him that I had a few buddies who could take care of them. "Well, give them a call and get the barbecue ready. Put on a pot of beans and I'll be over in about an hour." As luck would have it, I called everyone I knew and could reach no one, so when Slim arrived it was just him and me. I managed to polish off two elk steaks and a few beans, and you guessed it, Slim ate the rest.

Every once in a while I would get a call at eleven or twelve o'clock in the evening from Slim on his way home from a shoot. It would almost always start with "Hey Al, what you doing, you hungry? Let's meet down at Bill Lee's and have something to eat." Bill Lee's was one of Bakersfield's oldest Chinese restaurants and at that time it was open twenty-four hours a day. I would almost always drive the forty-five miles and meet him there and most of the time we were the only ones there except for the restaurant personnel. I am not kidding when I tell you that Slim would order one of everything on their menu. We would sit for hours sometimes talking about history or listening to Slim tell tales about thing that happened to him while working on various films. So many times I wished I had a tape recorder to preserve some of those great stories. When the food was served, everything stopped and the eating began, I don't think I have ever seen anyone who could pack away so much Chinese food as fast as Slim could… He could really eat!

During the filming of Sam Peckinpah's film, "The Getaway," a funny thing happened. We had filmed in San Marcos, Texas for a number of weeks and then made a location move to El Paso to finish the film. I knew Slim was due to work on the show our first week there, and sure enough one afternoon there was a knock at my door. It was Slim. He greeted me with, "Hey Al, come on. A friend of mine owns a great steak house here in town and has invited us for dinner." I told him that was great, but I had to be back early because I had a four o'clock call in the morning. Off we went. Slim was greeted by the owners, and we were treated to a great meal and a few drinks, then a few more drinks. It seemed that everyone there wanted to buy Slim a drink and it got later and later.

I'm not much of a drinker, so I was getting a bit more stupid with each round. There was a big tough Indian gal working as a waitress who kept making eyes at me and the more drinks I had the better she looked. At two a.m. in the morning they closed the joint but told everyone that they could stay a bit longer. All evening long the owner had prodded Slim to get on the small stage with the band and sing his version of the old western song, "The Strawberry Rhone." After who knows how many tequila shooters, Slim was ready. He got on the stage and began to sing. Slim is a great actor but not too much of a singer, but he gave it hell and the shooters still came. He then broke into the dirty version of the song which everybody loved and encouraged him to do more, and being an accommodating sort of a guy, he did.

While that was going on the waitress came over and sat down with me and whispered sweet nothing in my ear and told me how much fun we could have. I guess I just wasn't drunk enough to go for that but seemed to be trapped into a situation. The one thing I knew was I had to get back to my room and get a few hours' sleep. I told Slim I was going to get a cab back to the motel and would see him later in the day for he had a late call.

As I was leaving the waitress stopped me and wanted to come up to my room for some fun and games. I thought, *I have to figure a way out of this mess,* so I quickly formed a plan—not a good one but a plan. I told her that I had to get some sleep but to come to my room in a few hours and we would get together. She seemed to go for it and asked for my room number... I gave her Slim's.

After a few very short hours of sleep I arrived on set. I got a shot of vitamin B-12 and an upper from our on-set medic and was almost ready for the day's shooting. That afternoon when Slim reported to the set, he was sporting a pretty nice black eye. I asked him what happened. "It's your fault," he said. "That damn Indian showed up at my door drunk as a skunk looking for you. When I told her you were on the set she called me a bunch of names and then poked me in the eye... Sorry about that Slim!

Almost every time Slim stopped by, I would hear him pull into my driveway in his big cowboy truck. As soon as he got out, I would hear him shout, "Hey Al, you home?" It always made my day. Slim was one of those people who made me happy and I knew I would hear some wonderful jokes and good stories. I noticed that he always wore his spurs. I don't know how many of you have tried to drive wearing spurs, but it ain't easy. I asked him one day why he wore spurs while driving. He just grinned at me and said, "Oh shucks, it's what everybody expects to see!"

Through the years we had some great times that I will always cherish. Slim was always one of my best friends. When Slim passed away in 1983 it hit me hard, It happened so quickly none of us were prepared for it. One of the biggest honors of my life was when Maggie Pickens, Slim's wife, called and asked me to come to Pinedale, Wyoming to help with services for Slim. I left the next day with my girlfriend and made the long drive to Pinedale in record time. We sat with Maggie and his two daughters and discussed what they had in mind.

Knowing I had a bit of knowledge of the Plains Indian cultures, they asked if I knew anything about the ceremonies the Blackfoot people did for their departed loved ones. I explained that traditionally the ashes were placed in a bag made from the skin of the last animal taken by the deceased. Friends and family spread the ashes to the four corners, each saying a prayer as they did.

I asked if they had any skins or hides that Slim had taken recently from which I could make a bag. They brought me a small deer hide that had just come from the tanners. I looked at the small hide and the box containing Slim's ashes. I didn't think it would be big enough, but would give it a try. I excused myself and went to my cabin and began sewing up the hide. When it was done, I called Maggie and his daughters over to fill it. It was amazing, every bit of ash fit as if Slim had been guiding us, it was a perfect fit.

A few miles from Slim's ranch was his favorite hunting spot, an elk camp high in the mountains. That was where the family wanted to spread his ashes. Arrangements were made to take some of Slim's closest friends to the camp site by helicopter for a wake and services the next morning. A few of us rode to the camp on horseback, taking turns carrying the ash bag, our last ride with Slim. We laughed and shed a few tears as we related some of our personal stories about Slim. We arrived in camp a few hours later after a beautiful ride through the Wyoming high country.

That evening we had a great dinner of elk steaks, cooked over an open fire, and beans, Slim's favorite. After dinner and a few drinks we told Slim stories for hours, had some laughs and shed a few more tears. It was a gathering Slim would have liked. I told Maggie that we should find a good spot for the service. We walked outside in the bright moonlight and I ask if Slim had a favorite spot or place he talked about that might work. Maggie smiled and said he always talked about sitting in the outhouse watching the elk down by the pond. It seemed to be his favorite spot. We took a short walk to the outhouse and surveyed the area, nice flat ground with a gently rolling slope down to the pond. Perfect! We agreed that would be something he would like; we had found our spot.

Now this may sound like a tall-tale, but it is absolutely true. I asked the local archeologist, who was with us at the camp, if they had ever found any artifacts in these mountains. He said that it was very rare to find anything up this high, most everything was found below in the valleys or flat lands. Here is what happened.

When we walked back to the main camp, I noticed something lying on the ground just in front of the outhouse. I reached down and picked it up, it was a perfect flint spearhead. Being one who believes in ways of the old people and spiritual things, I got goose bumps as I handed it to Maggie. I thought Slim had sent us a message, you must keep this. It is a sign. It makes no sense that a beautiful artifact was laying right on the ground in front of the outhouse that had been used hundreds of times with all the foot traffic that had come and gone around it. There was only one explanation I came up with, Slim put it there as a sign that he approved.

The next morning at sun-up we all gathered together for the ceremony. I explained that as each person was handed the bag, they should say a prayer for Slim, spread some of the ashes to the four corners, and then hand it to the next person. As the last ashes were emptied and everyone had said their good-byes, from far away in the mountains came the mournful cry of a coyote and two hawks began circling the camp. It was a wonderful sign, and I don't think there was a dry eye in camp that morning. It is one hundred percent true, I have made nothing up. It happened just that way.

We all miss Slim. He was a very special person, and I look forward to meeting him again; we still have trails to blaze!

NAKIA

In 1972 I was in New Mexico working on a pilot for a new television series called, "Nakia," starring Robert Forester and Arthur Kennedy. It was the story roughly taken from the film "Billy Jack" of an Indian police officer. The major part of the filming was done in or around Albuquerque, New Mexico. We had a really good cast and crew who worked well together so there was always a lot of fun on the set. We raced against the winter weather that was bearing down on us.

During the shoot, we moved our location to Bernalillo, New Mexico, which at that time, was a small Indian and Hispanic town. That day the weather finally caught up with us. It rained and snowed all day, so we did most of our filming inside the local police station. We had a very critical outdoor night shot that we needed to get done before moving to another location. After we had shot everything we could inside, the decision was made to wait until dark and see if the weather let up enough that we could get our outdoor shot.

There was a small Mexican restaurant not far from where we were. A group of us decided to hang out there, have a few drinks and a bite to eat and wait for a break in the storm. We all met in Robert's trailer and, of course, Arthur had some of his now famous weed. Arthur liked to smoke a bit of grass all the time and always had the best in the area. After the pipe was passed around a few times, we went to the little restaurant to wait out the weather. About two hours and a lot of tequilas later, the First Ad came and told us they were ready to do the shot. We were a bit of a mess but a very happy lot, none of us felt any pain. We were anxious to get the shot done and get back to our warm hotel rooms and rest.

The shot we needed was rioters protesting at a local Indian mission. Robert and Arthur were to speed into the shot with sirens blaring, jump out, and arrest a few protesters. Easy shot, right? As luck would have it, the director asked me if I would play one of the leaders of the mob being I was a big burly looking guy with a beard. I was glad to do it for it meant another pay check, and the shot seemed easy enough. In the scene Robert and Arthur would roar into the shot, Robert would jump out, grab me, throw me across the hood of the squad car, handcuff me and put me into the car, easy enough.

We rehearsed the shot a few times and then were ready to do a take. The director called for action and all hell broke loose. The extras went into their rehearsed action as protesters and started raising hell and creating a mob scene. Robert and Arthur came into the shot full speed and promptly ran me over, mashed my big ass into the ground. The director screamed cut and everybody ran to where I lay in the mud. All I remember was Arthur, who had been driving, was kneeling next to me holding my head in his hands. He was almost crying and told me that he could not see me when they turned the big arc lights on because they blinded him.

The medic on the set showed up in short time and asked me if I could feel my feet or wiggle my toes. I told him I could and that I didn't think I was hurt too badly. They helped me to my feet, and believe it or not, I was in pretty good condition for a guy who had just been run over by a police car. I was saved by the weather. The rain and snow had turned the ground into a mush and the weight of the car just mashed me into the soft ground without doing any real damage except for a few bruises.

It worked well though. I got a lot of pats on the back and attention and a good pay check. Hell, I was a hero (for at least five minutes). So all was well! I did learn an important lesson. Never do any kind of stunt work with a stoned drunk actor behind the wheel of a speeding car!

The filming of "Nakia" will always hold a special place in my heart, not only because it was a great job with a great cast and crew, but I met a lady there who brought a long lasting love into my life.

ANNA AND THE KING

In the summer of 1972 I was at Twentieth Century Fox studio preparing to start a television series called "Anna and the King," starring Yul Brynner and dear friend, Samantha Eggar, which was based on the movie also starring Yul Brynner. The problem was that we were filming during the summer slowdown season in Hollywood when the studios close down for a few months while they air their new shows. Because of that, our crews were older employees of Fox Studios who were kept on salary by the studio because of seniority. In other words, we worked with a bunch of old grumpy farts who were just putting in their hours.

Luckily Yul and Samantha both had a great sense of humor and liked to have fun while shooting the long hours we had to put in on the show. As the weeks drug by we felt like we were working with the walking dead. There was no fun, just grumpy old men who complained and grumbled about one thing or the other. Also playing into our growing boredom was the fact that we only left the sound stage one time in the six weeks we had filmed... We went across the street and shot in the park. I tell you that being inside a big dusty sound stage every day on the same set got to us. We had to do something to break the boredom.

Because the studio was on short staff, the commissary on

the lot had only a skeleton crew working and a very limited menu. After eating there a couple of times, we decided that was not for us. It was worse than a military mess hall, the food was awful! At that time there were a couple of young girls who had started a catering business called The Movable Feast. They took orders and delivered them the next day when we broke for lunch. That turned out to be good for us, and we took our lunches to Yul's suite of rooms, had a nice leisurely lunch with a few glasses of wine, and got away from the crew for a while. Yul liked the finer things in life and did most of them to excess. He always had the best wine and drugs that money could buy. While we had lunch, he lit up a number, and we had a few hits. It helped us take the edge off when we had to go back to the set with our zombie crew. So that was our routine for most of the show.

One very difficult morning of shooting, with a lot of tension and uneasiness on the set, things were about to get ugly when they called for an early lunch break. Samantha and I knew Yul was about to break from the pressure put on him by the studio, and there was one thing you did not want to see, Yul (The King) snap! He was a wonderful kind man, but he was The King. He conducted himself that way and was larger than life, when he wanted something, he got it! That day he knew he had to do something to ease the tension on the set and breathe some life into the crew...

He came up with an idea. He sent his driver to get a few packages of ready-made chocolate chip cookie mix and a couple extra bags of chocolate chips. He asked me to stay in the suite when we were called back from the lunch break and bake a few dozen cookies for the crew. I agreed that I would do anything to not have to go back on stage for a while. He handed me a very large bag of marijuana and said, "Throw this in with the cookie mix." I thought he was joking at first but then realized he was dead serious, so that is what I did.

About an hour later I had two dozen beautiful looking

chocolate chip cookies ready to take to the set. I covered them with aluminum foil and headed for the sound stage. I found Yul and showed him my beauties and asked him what I should do with them. He told me to set them by the coffee urn and walk away. Sam, Yul and I each took a couple , then sat back and watched as various crew members picked up one or two and went to their work areas. We had a few good laughs about what was about to happen as we watched them devour the cookies.

In a short time our crew, which before had been like the walking dead, turned into the happy-go-lucky, fun loving, grab-ass crew we had hoped for. We heard comments from them about how much fun they were having and what a strange day it was... Of course they did not know that they were stoned out of their friggin' minds. It was a fun day for all and seemed to break the tension. I know it helped Yul for we all thought he would kill himself with laughter watching them that day.

The very next day the shit hit the fan. The producers and studio big shots were waiting for Yul to make his appearance when we arrived. We knew that was not a good sign and something was up, for none of them looked very happy. They immediately pulled Yul aside and took him to a darkened corner of the stage. Sam and I heard the ass chewing he got and wondered what was going down. After a while he returned with a big grin on his face. "Everything's okay," he said with a laugh. "It seems that everything we shot yesterday was not usable and the big wigs wanted to know what happened. So I told them what we did and why." That day cost Yul over twenty thousand dollars because he offered to pay for the day's shooting cost.

We finally finished the series and it is all history now. Looking back I guess there were some good times working on it, I just couldn't remember them. For me, being able to work with one of the greats like Yul Brynner and my good friend Samantha Eggar was the highlight of the whole thing.

STAR TREK

In 1984 I was at Paramount Studios working on a Star Trek movie called "The Search for Spock." It was like reliving some of my earlier days as a make-up artist for I had worked on the television series back in the late 1960s. Things had changed a lot since those early days, everything was bigger and more refined including some of the cast.

A make-up artist's day usually started at three or four in the morning, so our nights and sleep were very short. I was amazed to see groups of loyal Star Trek fans or Trekkies as they are called gathered at both gates all night long just to get a glimpse of the actors on the show… I guess that's what you call loyalty. I will tell you another story about this later.

The reason we had such early calls was that some of our make-ups took up to three, and sometimes four, hours to complete and shooting always started at seven. My routine was to report to the dark sound stage where the make-up tables were set up and get everything ready for the arrival of my first actor or stuntman. If I had time, I grabbed a roll and cup of coffee from the Craft Service man to get my heart started. The area where we worked was right next to the stars' trailers that served as dressing rooms. At that time in the morning the stage was completely dark except in our work area and the Craft Service area.

Every morning as I waited for my first victim, I noticed a little stout balding man walk by in the shadows and go into one of the dressing rooms. After seeing him a few mornings I thought it was a bit odd and mentioned it to one of the other make-up men on the show. He laughed and told me that the little fat man I was seeing was none other than William Shatner, the star of the show. I argued with him that it could not be Shatner, I knew him from working on the original series. "That was nearly eighteen years ago," he replied. "Just keep an eye on the dressing room and see who comes out later." Sure enough a few hours later out stepped Mr. Shatner or I should say Captain Kirk. It surely was magic what a hair piece and a girdle did to transform a toad into a prince.

It was amazing to see all of the behind-the-scenes magic that went into making the new Star Trek features. I must say I was fascinated with the entire process, how things had changed in eighteen years! It was a real pleasure working with the original cast from the old show. They had formed a real family-like bond with each other and seemed to be having a good time, all except the star.

For some unknown reason there was a real separation between most of the original actors on the show and Mr. Shatner, which became apparent when I ask them all to sign a publicity photo for me. Paramount had taken a nice group photograph of the crew that I thought would be nice to have. Everyone was very nice and signed it with no problem. Walter Koenig, who played Chekov, told me he didn't think Mr. Shatner would sign the same photo with the rest of the crew. He was right. I gave the photo to his make-up man to have him sign and was told he would have him sign a separate photo, Mr. Shatner would not sign a group shot. I thought that was a bit weird, but we were in Hollywood and sometimes weird is normal. I did get my signed group shot of the crew and a nice signed head shot from Mr. Shatner.

Now back to the Trekkies at the gate. One morning after shooting all night, I stopped at the main gate to talk to some of the fans waiting there. I wanted to know what they were doing there and why. After talking to some of them I was amazed to learn just how devoted to the show these fans were. Some had gone so far as to learn the Klingon language and to dress as Klingons. That was all pretty weird to me!

Almost all of the fans waiting there asked me if I had anything from the show that I would sell. Being a bit of a joker at times, I thought I would have a little fun with them. Very seriously I told them that I had a call sheet (call sheets were handed out at the end of the day's shooting to let the crew know what the next day's schedule was . . . most were thrown away after reading them). The crowd surged forward, and everyone wanted to buy it. At first I thought they had turned the tables on me and were having a joke at my expense, but soon realized that they were serious and really wanted to buy my call sheet. I handed it to one of the fans and started to leave. I was almost to my car when young man stopped me and told me that he would pay five dollars for each call sheet I gave him.

Well needless to say, each day when we wrapped, I gathered up all of the discarded call sheets I could find and sold them to him. That went on for the entire show. I have no idea how much extra cash I picked up but it was in the hundreds of dollars. I thought I had skinned a fat hog until years later when I went to a Star Trek convention and saw original call sheets sold for fifty dollars and up.

In 1986 I helped on another Star Trek movie called "The Voyage Home" and watched the special effects and set dressing crews turn the Paramount parking lot into San Francisco Bay complete with whales and a crashed space ship.

I have always thought I was blessed to be a part of the Hollywood film industry and to be able to work with some of the most talented people in the world. At times I thought

I should be paying them to be there and be part of the magic of film making. Where in the world could a country boy see huge mechanical whales swimming in a parking lot filled with a few feet of water and get paid for it?

WILD BILL

I have always had good luck through my life, which proved itself true again in the summer of 1995. While attending an antique swap meet in Ventura, California I had a chance meeting with a man named Danny Moore who was a costume designer for director Walter Hill. He was getting ready to start a film called "Wild Bill," the story of famous frontiersman and gunfighter, William Butler Hickock or Wild Bill Hickock as most knew him. He was looking for items he could use to make the film.

We got into a conversation about westerns and he asked me if I had any sources for correct period western items or material. Since I had been involved in some of the early westerns as an actor and stuntman, and had been a sort of historian on the west, I was able to give him some pretty good leads. Danny mentioned he was having Western Costume make all of the leather clothing that Jeff Bridges (Wild Bill) would wear in the film. I had seen some Western Costume leather work before in other films, and I guess I must have made a face or wrinkled my nose when he mentioned them because he asked me what was the matter. I was honest and told him that most of the things I had seen come out of Western looked manufactured or machine made and did not have the look of a handmade garment that Bill should have.

Then came a question which led me into a completely new phase of the film industry that I never had any idea I would be involved in. The question was, "Who would you recommend to make the clothing, if not Western?"

I jumped right in and said, "Me, I can make them!" We set up a meeting the next week at Danny's office to talk about what I could do and to show him some samples of things I had made.

At the meeting he looked at the things I brought in and we talked at length about what he needed. I knew he took everything I told him with a grain of salt for, as you know, Hollywood is full of con men and bull shitters out to make a fast buck in the film industry. Dan asked me if I could do some work for him that day. I knew he was testing me, so of course I agreed. He asked me to apply some fancy leather trim and designs to a pair of buckskin gloves. *No sweat*, I thought. *This will be a breeze.* So I began and made sure I did my best work. Everything went smoothly until I realized that I had screwed up big time. I had put the wrong trim on each glove, the right glove now had the left trim on it and the left had the right. I was in a panic as I tried to figure out how to make it right. I knew I had to fix them before Dan returned and saw my screw-up but was not fast enough. Danny stood there looking over my shoulder. I must have looked like a kid caught with his hand in the cookie jar as I sheepishly told him of my screw-up, I offered to stay all night to correct it and have it ready the next day.

That was how our first work day together went, not too smooth, but it all worked out. He gave me a design for a coat and asked me to make a sample, giving me a free hand to add anything I thought might look good on it. In a few days I returned with the coat, all handmade and aged down to look as though it had been around a while. He seemed impressed with what I had done and promptly gave me an order for two more coats. He set up a meeting with Walter Hill and Jeff Bridges to discuss the costumes Jeff would wear in the film. At that point I thought, *What have I gotten myself into, can I pull this off, this is the big time, am I really going to be able to deliver?* I had all kinds of questions and the only answer I came up with was to go ahead and give it a try! So that's what I did.

At the meeting I just hung back and let Danny do most of the talking and only opened my big mouth when I was asked a direct question. After the meeting Jeff asked me if I knew anything about tracking or hunting. I told him I had a bit of knowledge in that field. He asked me if I would show him the basics of tracking; he had a scene in the film where he had to be a tracker. I agreed to show him what I knew. Being a guy who liked a good practical joke and wanting to break the ice to see if Jeff had a sense of humor, I went into my act as a tracking instructor. Remember we were in a room with the director, the producer, the costume designer and a couple of other guys.

I had Jeff get down on his knees and sniff the ground, then pretend to pick up sand and let it slowly sift from his hand (in real life to see wind direction). I had him stand, put his hand above his eyes in a saluting manner and look to the left and right scanning the horizon, and sniff the air. At that point he knew I was screwing with him and a big grin came over his face. "You got me!" he said. Everyone in the room had a good laugh at Jeff's expense. I knew then he was a good guy who had a great sense of humor and would be a pleasure to work with. I made all the leather clothing Jeff wore in the film.

I also made clothing for Jim Gammon and Ellen Barkin. I will relate an amusing story about my first meeting with Miss Barkin. It was at Goldwyn Studios where we were filming the interior shots of the Number One Saloon. I had not yet met her but that day I needed to get her measurements so I could make her a leather Calamity Jane coat. I was directed to her dressing trailer. I knocked on the door and a young lady opened it. I told her why I was there and let her know that it would only take a few minutes. I was told Miss Barkin was busy but would be with me shortly. That sounded reasonable to me so I waited and waited. I could hear some grab-assing going on inside the trailer. It was a hot day so I knocked again and when the door opened I got a very snooty, "I told you Miss Barkin is busy and will be with you soon, just wait!" The door slammed.

I began to get a bit upset but held my temper as I waited outside in the heat. I waited for what seemed like hours but in reality was more like thirty minutes. I said to myself, *Screw this! I've had enough.* I banged on the door and was not very polite when it opened and the little groupie with an attitude stuck her head out, "I told you to wait until she is ready."

Before she could say another word I told her in no uncertain certain terms, all I needed was some simple measurements so the coat would fit right. I started to turn and walk away and added, "I'm getting paid the same if it fits or not and at this point I could give a damn less if it doesn't fit right." I headed for the main gate. Just as I was about to leave the studio one of her assistants came running after me and brought me back to do the measurements I needed to make the coat. I think it took all of ten minutes.

Sometimes in Hollywood the so-called stars get caught up in their own importance and forget the folks around them that make them look good on screen. Most of the time the little guy, and sometimes the studio, puts up with this self-indulgence and by doing so create their own monsters!

We finished filming "Wild Bill," and it was a first class shoot. Walter Hill, our director, made sure we had the best of everything. It was hard work, but I enjoyed every day on set. I thought we shot a really good film about Hickock as did everyone on the set. When we went to the screening we were shocked to see that a potentially great film had been screwed up in the editing room. Hollywood strikes again!

THE CHEROKEE KID

The "Cherokee Kid" seemed like one of those films that would be fun to do. It starred comic actor Sinbad and was a light hearted comedy set in the old west. After meeting with designer Dan Moore at Western Costume it sounded like a fun project, so I agreed to come on board. I would make leather costumes for the leads in the film along with various other items of wardrobe. That was great for me because I could do most of my work from my home studio and only had to be on set a few days.

Dan had set a fitting day with Sinbad and asked if I would be there to help design and get measurements to make a leather coat for him. When I arrived at the fitting, there were a lot of Sinbad's friends, along with production people, filling the room. I introduced myself and showed them my costume sketches with ideas for the coat. While they were going over them I noticed I was standing next to a very big black man. I didn't know who he was but thought I would make casual conversation with him and opened up with, "Damn you're tall enough to be a basketball player!" The whole room burst into laughter and the man gave me a dirty look and flashed the largest diamond ring I have ever seen in my face.

Sinbad came over to me, tears streaming down his cheeks from laughing so hard, and said, "That was a good one!" I still did not know what was so funny. I learned later the man was Shaquille O'Neal, the basketball player. Not being much of a sport fan I had no idea who he was.

The shoot on "Cherokee Kid" was a pleasant one with a lot of grab-assing and practical jokes and turned out to be a pretty good film. I had a chance to spend some time with old friend and Florida boy, Burt Reynolds, who I hadn't seen in years. I made him two character hats he wore in the film. Working with Sinbad was a real pleasure, he was funny, easy going and really took a liking to playing a cowboy. He became quite good with the Colt pistols he used in the film. The next time you see a Sinbad film notice there is never any vulgar language or anything that might offend anyone; he is a straight up nice guy. We were told that there would be a sequel to the film and everyone seemed very excited about it, but it never happened. I thought it was a cute little film and was fun to work on.

Dan Moore

I must thank my old friend Dan Moore for having faith in me and my ability to produce and design leather costumes and other wardrobe items. Because of Dan, I worked on a lot of films and made some things I was really proud of. I still see costumes that I made years ago being used in many of the western period films. He got me involved in an area of film making that I would have never considered if it weren't for him.

I had made a few things for films before I met Dan. I made leather costumes for "The Quick and the Dead" and "Indian in the Cupboard" but did those as a favor for a friend of mine. Dan was the one who really got me involved and made it fun (sometimes) to create things for the stars. Because of Dan, I went on and made the principle leather clothing for "Wild Bill," "The Cherokee Kid," "The Missing," and "The Magnificent Seven" (We won an Emmy for costume on that TV series. I also landed a recurring cameo part of the Buffalo Man in that series.)

The first time we worked together, I made the principle coat for Jeff Bridges in "Wild Bill." After aging it, I took it to Dan for his approval. He looked it over, gave it a thumbs

up, and asked me to give him an invoice so I could get paid. I made out what I thought was a professional looking invoice and gave it to him. He looked it over, handed it back to me and told me that I had to change it. I asked him what the problem was, not knowing what to change; I thought maybe I had charged too much for the work I had done. He looked at me very seriously and said, "Triple all your prices. You didn't charge enough."

I was very lucky to have met Dan Moore. I learned a lot from him and we had a lot of fun working together. In my opinion he is one of Hollywood's best costume designers. He has an eye for textures and designs that most of today's wardrobe people don't possess. The films he designs always have a special look that sets them aside from the usual Hollywood production. I am very lucky and proud to call him a friend.

ADVENTURES WITH SAM

As I mentioned earlier in the book, Samantha Eggar ("The Collector") is a dear friend of mine. We met in the late 1960s. I don't recall who introduced us or how we first met, but that's not important to this story. The first film we worked on together was a project called "The Grove," which was to be filmed in Vancouver, British Columbia. We met and discussed the project, and the fact that it was being done by an independent film company and the money was very good. She gave me a copy of the script to read. I took it home that night and read it a few times. The next morning I had a call from Sam asking me what I thought about the project. I explained that I had read it a few times but still did not know what the story was about. Well it turned out, she didn't either.

The story was about an old abandoned mansion on an island and a young couple who went there and went crazy. It rambled on and on with disconnected scenes and naked folks running about with no rhyme or reason. Remember it was the 1960s and there were a lot of artsy underground films showing up all over the country, so we both thought perhaps that was one of those off beat projects.

We agreed that if nothing else, it would be fun to work in Vancouver and the money was good, and we were paid in cash, even better! We signed on to the project and found out

THE GROVE MANSION

that Samantha's costar would be actor Robert Culp ("I Spy"), who I had worked with earlier on his series. So we went to British Columbia. Sam flew and I drove so I had wheels while we were there.

When we arrived we found that we were staying in a beautiful upscale hotel called The Bay Shore Towers, right on the bay across from Lionsgate Park. At our first production meeting we were informed that to get to our location we had two choices, one was to take the water taxi (a speed boat) which would take nearly two hours, or fly in on a small four-seater seaplane which would take about forty-five minutes. They told us that the plane ride could be dangerous because there were a lot of floaters in the water that time of the year. A floater was a log that had broken away from one of the logging outfits working in the remote parts of the river. They were hard to spot for they were just below the surface and could not be seen until it was too late.

The first morning we opted to take the water taxi and reported to the docks two hours earlier than our call. We grabbed coffee and some sweet rolls and were off. The ride to location was spectacular; dawn on the Indian Arm River was a thing of beauty. The river was parted by unspoiled wilderness of thick lush forests and waterfalls everywhere we looked, it was British Columbia at her best! As we neared our location we saw the island where we would be shooting and the old mansion that was our set.

It was an eerie looking old place that one could see had been a grand and beautiful mansion at one time. Indian Arm, as we called it, was built by Kaiser Wilhelm, the German leader, before World War One. It was to be his private hunting lodge and getaway, and he brought some of the finest and skilled woodworkers from Germany to do the construction and finish work. Just after the construction was finished, the war started and the property was taken over by the British Government. The building became an exclusive private club, then a hotel and gambling house, and then a house of ill repute. It was raided and closed by the Mounties in the 1940s and sat idle and abandoned since. Vandals and thieves had pretty much destroyed it and taken everything of value from the grand old building.

The company brought in large barges that provided dressing rooms and offices, and docked them at the pier near the mansion. That is where we would spend most of our time. The first morning Sam and I did some exploring around the island to see what was there, and we noticed an Indian tepee set up on one side of the old mansion, so we went to investigate. As we neared it, a bearded man with long hair dressed in the hippie style of that era stepped out.

When he saw me, he broke into a smile came over and gave me a big hug. To my surprise he said, "Al, how are you doing?" It was my old friend, Don Franks, who had been the star of a television series I had done at MGM called "Jericho." He had turned hippie and given up everything to live free in a tepee on the island with his wife and a young daughter. He had been hired to watch the location at night after the crews went home. It sure is a small world!

Everything about that job was crazy. The first few days all we did was go to the location, sit around, rehearse a few scenes, then sit around some more. The cameras had yet to arrive and no one seemed to do anything.

The first morning Robert Culp arrived on location, he had his own boat; he did not want to ride with us for some unknown reason. We all thought maybe he wanted to learn his lines or maybe he had first day jitters and wanted to be alone until he got to know everyone a little better. When he arrived, we all greeted him warmly as he passed us and went to his dressing room. He ignored us, went inside and closed the door. That should have told us something right off, but we dismissed it to first day jitters and we went about our business. For days we got the same cold snobbish attitude from him, like he thought he was better than the rest of us. Finally we had to concede that he was just an asshole with a big ego, so we just ignored him for the rest of the show.

As time progressed and no filming was done, we finally figured out what was going on. It was one of those scams that Hollywood is famous for. They had found some poor jerk who wanted to be in a movie, who had written a script and had more money than brains, and they were playing him. When he showed up one day to do his big scene, he was a nervous wreck. They had everything in place, cameras and lights were set up and ready. I felt a bit sorry for him, because all he did was run about naked making long rambling speeches that meant nothing. It was comical and sad at the same time to watch that poor fool make an ass of himself. After that he was full of himself. He was on the set every day watching and giving advice about how he wanted everything shot. Better than half the time there was no film in the cameras.

Each day after we wrapped, it was routine that I went back to the hotel and cleanup. I then went to Sam's room and we ordered meals brought up and sat on the balcony watching the boats in the harbor while we ate and had a glass of wine. It was a very relaxing way to wind down after a day on the set. One evening she got a call from actor Warren Beatty while we were finishing our meal. He was her friend and he was going to stop by to say hello.

When he arrived she introduced him, and he was very cold and seemed a bit upset to see me there. As the time passed he became even more upset and became rude. I thought maybe I was in the way and he wanted to be alone with Sam, so I excused myself. But after thinking about it a while, I think I know what happened. You may know Beatty considers himself quite a ladies' man and rumors have it that he has bedded most of the actresses in Hollywood. He most likely planned to add Sam to that list and I was in the way that night.

After a few weeks on location, we all started to get bored for there was nothing to do on the island once we had explored it from one end to the other. One morning Don Franks asked us if we knew about the wild magic mushrooms that grew wild in Lionsgate Park. We told him we knew nothing about them, so he explained that every morning at sun-up there was a race between the hippies and the mounted police to see who got to them first. He explained that it was not illegal to pick them; you just had to be fast. We thought what the heck we have nothing to lose, so we gave it a try.

Bright and early the next morning we had our driver take us to the park. All sorts of people and the mounted police ran madly through the park frantically picking mushrooms as fast as they could. It was a scene right out of some mad-cap movie and everyone was having fun. It didn't take us long to join in on that wonderful game. We picked mushrooms as fast as we could find them and ended up with a nice little bag full.

That morning we decided to take the plane, instead of the water taxi, to location. It was a beautiful trip for the wilderness around Vancouver is breathtaking, to say the least. Our pilot told us the history of the river as he pointed out various sites along the way. As we neared the location he told us that our landing might be a bit rough because of a cross wind that created the white caps on the water, but not to worry, he had done this hundreds of times. Down we went for our first seaplane landing. As the plane pontoons hit the water things indeed got rough, and we were bounced around pretty good. Then all of a sudden there was a loud boom and the plane lurched forward, took to the air again and almost nose-dived into the water, we thought we were goners. The pilot got control of the plane again and informed us that we had just hit a floater. That was the last time we flew to location!

Upon arrival we were anxious to show Don our little bag of mushrooms so went directly to his tepee. One would have thought we had brought him a bag of gold. He quickly had his wife prepare a few and instructed us how to use them. We each ate only one, not knowing what the effect would be, for we had the workday ahead of us. When the first assistant director arrived, he told us that it would be a few hours before we did anything so we could just hang out and relax. It was a good thing because the effects of our magic mushrooms were just starting to hit us.

Earlier that week I had discovered an old dump site on the back side of the island and had found a few old bottles and other interesting things. I told Sam that I was going there to do some serious digging for artifacts and if they needed me that's where I would be. I borrowed a shovel from our prop man and off I went. By then the mushrooms had turned me into a very jolly fellow and the hike to the dump site was magical. I dug and from the first shovelful I found wonderful things from the early days of the old mansion. Everything was a treasure; I had hit the mother lode. Of course a lot of it was just junk, but in my mushroom soaked mind, it was treasure.

It seemed like I was there for hours when I heard voices behind me. Sam, Don and his wife were also frantically digging, and they had been there quite some time for they had piles of artifacts, too. We dug until they came and got us for lunch. We were a sight covered from head to toe with dirt and grime, and looked like a bunch of coal miners. We spent many fun hours digging for treasure and did find some very nice early artifacts and bottles. It was a good getaway from the boredom and slow process of that film. It was also the last time we ate mushrooms!

As the film wound down, Sam's part came to an end and we were all ready for a change. We had some good times and had made very good money on the project, but it was time to move on. Near the last day of shooting Mr. Culp approached me and was very nice (for the first time sense he arrived). He asked me to stay another few days to do his girlfriend's make-up for her part in the film. I told him that I had plans to go to Alaska for a little vacation and would not change them. He offered me quite a bit of money to stay just a few days and work with her. That was when I told him what an unprofessional asshole I thought he had been to Sam and me throughout the film and that he did not have enough money to get me to stay. I was off to Alaska to drive until all roads ended.

I went on to do several films with Samantha, "Anna and the King," "Why Shoot the teacher?" "The Hand," "The Legendary Curse of the Hope Diamond," and "The Grove." She is a great actress and a lot of fun to work with; we had many adventures on and off film. She is a great lady and one of my best friends.

OTHER FUNNY TIDBITS
THAT YOU MIGHT FIND AMUSING

ROY ROGERS

From the time I was a small young lad, I was a Roy Rogers fan as most boys were in those days. We saw every film he made and could not wait to get to the theatre Saturday morning to see the next one. Our bicycles became Trigger, we wore white cowboy hats and well-worn cap pistols and we kept our neighborhoods safe from the villains who lurked behind every tree and garage. It was a wonderful time before computers, when kids used their imaginations to create worlds of wonder and fun.

When I came to Hollywood I had always wanted to meet him but never had the chance. While working at the Corriganville Movie Ranch one of the stuntmen told me that there was a junk shop in Chatsworth called O'Shea's Trash and Treasures. It was run by an old retired character actor named Jack (Blackjack) O'Shea who had played the heavy in many of the old western movies. I made a point to find the shop and meet O'Shea. It was just the type of shop I loved, full of worthless junk mixed in with some real treasures, with character everywhere I looked with no rhyme or reason to anything.

The minute I met Jack, I knew him—from all of the westerns I had watched as a kid. He was a real character who always wore an old beat up black wide brimmed Stetson cowboy hat, still had his jet black handlebar mustache, and almost always wore a well-worn western vest. Over time I got to know him pretty well for I became a regular at his shop. I loved it. There was always some old stuntman or actor hanging around talking about the good old days. I sat there for hours listening to stories about actors they had worked with and great western films they had taken part in. Most of the time there was a bottle of Jack Daniels or some other cheap whisky passed around, which improved the stories as it made its rounds.

I found out that Roy Rogers had bought the shop for Jack as a retirement gift and occasionally helped him out when thing got tough. I mentioned to Jack that I had always wanted to meet Roy but had never had the chance. In Jack's usual fashion he told me, "Don't worry, kid. I will call you the next time Roy stops by and you can come over meet him." Well time went by and then one day Jack called and told me to get over as fast as I could, that Roy was there. I quickly changed into my best western clothes and made a record breaking trip to Jack's shop, couldn't wait to meet Roy after all those years. Upon arrival I saw only Jack's old pickup truck parked in front of the shop, and when I entered there was nobody there except Jack. I thought, *Shit I missed him!* I was very disappointed, to say the least, and I guess Jack saw that on my face.

He looked at me and smiled, "He's in the back room. You'll meet him in a few minutes." My mood changed from disappointment to excitement, I was finally going to meet one of childhood heroes. I could not wait. The phone rang. Jack answered it and said, "We'll be right over. Well, come on back and meet Roy," he said as he led me toward the back room. My heart beat faster with excitement; I was finally going to meet Roy Rogers. We entered the small dark back room and I could hardly see, then as my eyes adjusted to the dark. Roy lay passed out on a small bed, drunk as a skunk, out like a light. "Roy likes to have a few belts once in a while. Grab his feet," Jack said.

"What do you mean?" I ask him.

"We're going to take him home. Come on. Help me get him to the truck." We hauled Roy to Jack's old pickup, laid him on an old mattress in the bed of the truck and headed off. We pulled up at the Rogers' ranch and were met by Dale and two others who unloaded Roy and carried him to the house. He never opened his eyes or made a sound all the time I was there. So I had still not met Roy.

Many years later I did get to spend some time with him shooting skeet and trap and we had a good laugh about the good old times at Jack's little shop. He was a great guy and is still one of my heroes.

HOLLYWOOD TOUGH GUY

In the latter part of 1966 I met one of Hollywood's top villains and tough guy, Leo Gordon, the only man who could claim he had played in a mud puddle with John Wayne (in the film "McClintock"). We hit it off right away because of our interests in military history and my knowledge of the World War Two German Africa Corp. At that time Leo was polishing up his script "Tobruk" that Universal Studios had picked up and was getting ready to start filming. We spent a lot of time in the Review Studio Commissary discussing various things that he wanted to put into the film.

After a few weeks of meetings, he invited me to a party he hosted at his house in the valley. He told me there would be a lot of studio people and it would be a good time to meet some of the folks. I was excited and could not wait for the weekend to roll around and thought, *Wow! My first really Hollywood party, this is going to be a blast!* I followed the map and directions Leo had given me and I found his house with no problem. The valley, at that time, was horse property and small ranches. I pulled into the driveway and saw quite a few cars and heard music coming from the house. I parked my car, went up to the house and knocked on the door.

Leo greeted me and invited me inside which was pretty dark, and it took my eyes a bit to get use to the dim surroundings. As my eyes adjusted I could not believe what I saw. There were naked folks everywhere engaged in everything you can imagine and some you could not. I guess I was still a shy country boy for that scared the daylights out of me. I had heard about Hollywood parties but thought it was just another story. Leo laughed when he saw the look on my face. "Don't worry," he said, "Everyone is very friendly. Make yourself at home." Friendly! I guess so. Like home? I don't think so or at least not at my home.

That was really not my thing so I wandered around for a while, took in all the sights, and when the time was right made my escape. It was quite an experience for a country boy, and I must say I did learn a few things! For years after, Leo and I had quite a few laughs about it and how naive and green I was in those days.

HERO

It's not too often in life that we get the chance to meet a real hero. My chance came in the summer of 1975. I was hired to do make-up on a commercial for Chrysler that was filmed at the small Producers Studio in Hollywood. The commercial company had hired the first man to walk on the moon, Neil Armstrong, to be their spokesman.

I was excited to meet Mr. Armstrong. It's not every day one gets to meet a real astronaut who walked on the moon.

After getting set up for his arrival, I got a cup of coffee to get myself going and ready for my first victim. While talking with some of the other crewmen, someone behind me asked if I was Mr. Fleming. I turned around, and it was Mr. Armstrong. He introduced himself (like I didn't know who he was). We shook hands and he got himself a cup of coffee and came back and joined our little group. He was just one of the guys telling jokes and blending in with the rest of us earthlings.

I did his make-up and he confided in me that he was a bit nervous about doing a commercial. I assured him that it was a might easier than going to the moon. I did my best to put him at ease, which is one of the jobs of a make-up artist. They soon called for a rehearsal.

I think everyone on the crew saw that he was ill at ease when he did his first walk-through; he had trouble remembering his dialog and was not comfortable with all the lights, equipment and crew around him. After quite a few rehearsals the director called for our first take of the morning. It was a disaster. Neil could not get his dialog right and kept blowing his lines. As was true with a lot of actors when they goofed up their lines, panic sets in and every time they got to a certain point in the dialog that gave them trouble, they went blank. I felt sorry for him. I knew what he was going through. After many takes we got nowhere so our director called for an early lunch break to give Neil sometime to regain his composure.

I saw his frustration and embarrassment as he went to his dressing room, and I felt bad for him. Having had some acting experience and training, I thought I might be able to help him with some of the tools I had learned. I decided to give it a try and went to his dressing room and knocked on his door, he invited me in. I explained in a nice professional way that I might be able to help him remember his lines with a tool I had learned from my acting coach a few years ago.

He was eager to learn, so we spent the next hour going over a method called the key word system used by a lot of actors in Hollywood.

The system is based on the key word in the dialog, in this case "Chrysler," and what it does or why you are talking about it. It is a pretty easy system when learned, and Neil picked it up easily after we practiced it a few times. While talking I had to ask him, "How did it feel to be on the moon?"

He looked at me with a slight grin and answered, "Lonesome!" When the crew returned from the lunch and we began shooting again everything went fine. Neil breezed through his dialog with little problem.

At the end of the shoot he came over to me and thanked me for my help and asked if there was anything he could do for me. I thought for a minute, "I sure would like an autographed photo if you have one."

He told me that he did not have any with him but as soon as he returned home he would see that I got one. Most of the time when someone asks a famous person or a star for an autographed photo, and they tell you that they will send one, you will never get it. As a professional make-up artist I seldom asked for autographed photos. But twice in my career I have, because I respected the person I was working with and wanted something to remember them by. Bob Hope was one of those people and Neil Armstrong the other. I guess I was lucky for both sent the requested photograph.

A few weeks after working with Neil Armstrong, a package arrived at my studio. It held a beautiful color photograph signed to me of Neil in full space suit with the moon behind him, along with a block of postage stamps with his image also signed, and an Omega wristwatch with a note saying that it was one of four watches he took with him to the moon. Needless to say these items are some of my prized possessions. It was a real honor to have worked with Neil Armstrong, a real American hero, and with his recent passing America has lost one of our best!

TIPTOEING THROUGH THE TULIPS WITH TINY TIM

Earlier I mentioned I had a call to shoot an album cover for the offbeat singer, Tiny Tim, who was making a name for himself at that time. I had no idea what to expect as I went to the door of his modest apartment one evening. I knocked and was greeted by a nice, almost normal looking girl who introduced herself as Miss Vickie. I entered and the place looked like an explosion in a ribbon factory, there were brightly colored scarves and posters everywhere but no Tiny Tim. Miss Vickie excused herself and went into the other room and returned with Tim holding onto her arm. Well first off Tim was not tiny, he stood at least six foot six tall and weighed a good two hundred fifty pounds, and he was shaped like a big pear, small shoulders and big rear end. He was dressed in a wrinkled sport coat and baggy pants that looked as if they had not seen a washing in sometime.

Miss Vickie introduced me as the photographer who was going to shoot the new album cover. Tim slowly stuck out his hand but never looked at me. When I shook his hand it was like picking up a dead mackerel from the fish market, clammy and limp. I asked him if he had any ideas for the album cover. He whispered something to Miss Vickie and she told me that he wanted me to come up with something. I was on the spot so I suggested we listen to the new record to see if anything came to mind.

That seemed to delight Tim for he jumped up and squealed, and rushed over and put the record on the turntable, and it began to play. As it played, he danced around the room making faces, rolling his eyes, and making funny little noises listening to himself on the record. It was quite a show! The last song on the album ended and I had no idea what to do, not being a Tiny Tim fan I was at a loss to come up with an original idea. I thought maybe something in a nut house would be more appropriate but knew I could not say that, so I faked it. I began shooting anything I could think of just get the job done and get out of there. I shot four rolls of film, told them I thought I had what they needed, and would have a proof sheet ready the next day for their approval.

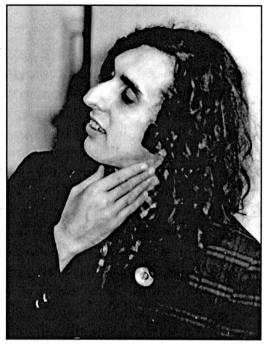

Miss Vickie told me Tim wanted to sing a new song he had just written to get my opinion of before I left. He brought out his little ukulele and began to play. I thought he was having a seizure for he began rolling his eyes and jumping up and down as he played and then he began to sing (in truth I don't think you could really call it singing), but I listened. What else could I do? After he stopped, he just stared at me and waited for some kind of response. As soon as I realized what he wanted, I broke into a smile and told him how much I liked it. He came over and threw his arms around me gave me a big hug. He said, "God bless you." That was the only thing he said to me that whole evening.

I sent my assistant over the next day with the proof sheet and the rest is history. To think I gave up a moment in history to spend the evening with Tiny Tim. As I mentioned earlier, I had press passes to be at the Roosevelt Hotel that night to continue my photo essay of Robert Kennedy.

REMEMBERING

As mentioned earlier, I spent most of my early years as a make-up artist at MGM Studios in Culver City, California. I was very lucky to and privileged to spend nearly fifteen years there as a young apprentice and then a full-fledged group one make-up artist. In those early days, MGM was a wonderful place to work, it was like one big family. Everyone knew each other and we were all happy. Our studio turned out some of the best films ever made in Hollywood and it had some of the best stars ever under contract.

The studio consisted of the main lot or lot one and lots two and three. Each lot had its own set, one was where all the big sound stages were, lot two had its western town and the mock-up of the ship "Bounty" in a big pond from the movie "Mutiny on the Bounty." Lot three had the European town blown all to hell that was the set for the television series "Combat."

The big make-up department was located in the producers' building on the main lot. We each had our personal make-up room in that building where everything started each morning. There was a waiting room at the entrance where actors waited to be called for their morning make-up before reporting to the stage. Coffee and rolls were located there, so it was the first place everyone headed when reporting for the day's work. There was an endless parade of stars and want-to-be stars there each morning and I met some wonderful characters.

I remember coming to work one morning and upon entering the room heard loud voices. Danny Thomas and Frank Sinatra were in a heated discussion about how much better and safer Las Vegas was when the mafia ran it than it was today. I, being the nosy type, got a cup of coffee and sat down and listened to what they said. After listening to Sinatra, I had to agree with him. He argued that in those days there was no beggars on the street, you never heard of a robbery or purse snatching, and if you did it was quickly and quietly taken care of by the boys and a new shallow grave showed up in the desert. I sat there fascinated by what he was saying and he looked over at me and said, "What do you think kid?"

What was I to say except, "You're right, Mr. Sinatra!"

I loved my years at MGM and can't think of a better place to have spent my early days in the film industry. I can't remember any other studio that had the friendly feeling that Metro had, the feeling of being a part of something, of being one big family. I can remember the day that everybody on the lot got a notice with their time card that the studio would be closing after we finished the projects we were working on. Nobody knew what happened for the studio was busy, every stage had productions going, our back lots were all being used, it was like a black cloud had fallen over Metro.

The atmosphere on the lot was sad. It was like our world had just fallen apart, everyone felt like they were losing a dear friend. Most of the departments told everyone that if they wanted anything they could have it because they were closing their doors for good in a few weeks and everything had to go.

I was working at the time on lot three on a series called "Jericho," about freedom fighters in France during World War Two. We were shooting right next to the old mock-up of the "Bounty" ship. I watched one day as a crew started destroying the old set. It was sad to watch that great old ship that MGM's craftsmen and artists had taken so much time building and all the fine details they had put into its construction. As I watched, I noticed that the crew had thrown a lot of wooden buckets and belaying pins into a pile next to a dumpster. I asked what they were going to do with them and was told that they were going into the big crusher that evening. I ask for a few buckets and an arm load of the belaying pins. I use the wooden handmade buckets from the good ship "Bounty" in my home and office as trash cans. I think of all the great costumes and props I could have had that were destroyed when Metro closed her doors. It is a crime what Hollywood did to some of its history Today collectors and some museums try to find and preserve some of that great era.

REVENGE OF A SOUNDMAN

Two different sound men told me this story and I believe it to be true. It is another example of why you should treat everybody with whom you work with respect or there could be repercussions. The story concerns a very well-known female singer with a beautiful voice a big nose and bad teeth who was very popular at that time. She was known to give everybody around her a hard time and make unreasonable demands. She was, and still is, very disliked by people who have to work around her.

The top sound and audio company in Hollywood had contracted to supply the microphones for her concert tours at that time and true to form she gave them problems and made demands far beyond normal. Everyone tried to please her, but nothing they did seemed to work. She was just a bitch and everyone hated to be around her.

As often happens in Hollywood, a plan was formulated for revenge. She demanded a certain brand of microphones that were to be sterilized and sealed in individual plastic bags for each of her shows. She proceeded to show them just how they had to be placed in the bag and just how the bag had to be sealed making it just as difficult as she could for them. Nobody wanted to work with or for her but a few poor souls had to do the job, and of course, nothing was ever right. After a few months of that, the crew was fed up with her and her ways, which brought the revenge.

Each time they packaged her microphones, instead of sterilizing them as demanded, they gave them a special preparation. They dropped their pants and rubbed the mike between the cheeks of their asses before sealing them in the plastic bag. So if you saw one of her concerts and she had tears in her eyes and a wrinkled-up nose it might not have been emotions. It was most likely from some odd fumes coming from her microphone!

Revenge is sweet in Hollywood!

THINKING BACK

I was thinking about how the world has changed since I was a kid back in the late 1940/50s. I worked all week cleaning horse stalls and feeding our horses to earn my shinny half dollar allowance. Saturday morning my eight year old sister and I would walk three blocks to the bus stop, ride the bus into the city, get off at the city park, and then walk another six blocks to the Roxy Theatre. I bought two tickets for the Saturday matinee, and stocked up on popcorn (buttered, of course) and various candies. We then settled down and watched two feature films, along with a couple serials, some cartoons and the news, all in good taste of course. In those days we had some great heroes that all kids looked up to and learned from. After the movies we headed back to the ranch. Remember all this was done on less than a half dollar, and we were in no danger at any time.

Today when you go to a movie you almost have to hock your house or sell your first born to afford it. When popcorn sells for five dollars a tub you know you are in trouble. Look who our kids have as idols today, mostly ego walking around trying to be cool with nothing of substance and no real life experiences, only empty suits. Today many actors and sports personalities should be doing time instead of being role models for our younger generation. It is no wonder that our kids are growing up with so many problems and no respect for themselves or anyone else. It's a different world out there today! Too bad for our kids.

PLANET OF THE APES 1968

It is not too often that a make-up artist gets a chance to be part of history, but that is what happened in the summer of 1968. Little did we know that the job we were working on would change the world of special effect make-up forever. That summer a few of us were hired by make-up genius, John Chambers, to help him with a new concept in special effect make-up he developed for a film called "Planet of the Apes." We worked in special make-up units that had been placed outside the regular make-up department at Twentieth Century Fox Studios.

Our job was applying experimental latex and rubber appliances, designed by Chambers, on actors who had been hired as models. For weeks we reported to the studio at five in the morning and worked until seven each night experimenting with appliances that Chambers had designed, trying to find a rubber that would allow the actors facial expressions to be seen under the make-up. It was hard long tedious work but it was even harder on the poor models who came in every morning and sat all day while we applied the new appliances we tested that day. Each evening we had to remove rubber make-up and glues we used from their faces. In those days we were using alcohol, acetone, and MEK to do that, we learned later those substances are very toxic.

After a few days many of our models faces were raw and inflamed from all the chemicals we used. The real heroes of all those experiments were those models who endured countless hours in a make-up chair and let us do whatever we needed to do to create the look we were striving to achieve. We tried to make it as easy as we could on them, but there is just no easy way to paint an actor's face with spirit gum or other adhesives we were using and testing. One must remember after we began to work on them, which took hours, they could no longer drink or eat anything unless through a straw. They earned every dollar they were paid.

It was great experience for young make-up artists to work with someone as talented as John Chambers. We all learned things that would eventually change the make-up industry. The amazing things you see today's make-up artists doing on screen can be directly attributed to Chambers early work and experiments we did that summer so many years ago. John Chambers won an Oscar that year for best make-up effects as well as many other awards.

An amazing thing that none of us knew in those days was Chambers also worked very closely with the CIA and other government agencies to help keep our country safe. He was truly a genius and a true American original. I was very privileged to be able to call him a friend and to work and learn from him.

A FUNNY THING HAPPENED IN HOLLYWOOD

Here is a funny little story that kind of relates to Hollywood and the movie industry.

Back in the early seventies a good friend and writing partner, William O'Hagen, and I worked on a script idea. As many writers and film people did, we met in a local coffee shop to work on our story. It was a substitute office and an excuse to get out of the house. We got to know the waitresses and over time they became close friends, the fact that they were very good looking had nothing to do with it! As we got closer we would share jokes and stories with each other.

One afternoon one waitress wanted our advice about something. Some sleazy little guy came in and told her that he was a movie producer and wanted her to audition for him. Right away the red flags went up for we had all heard this story before. After all everyone in Hollywood was a big shot and was looking for the next big star or had the big movie deal. She did not like it but did not want to ruin a chance at a film role if the little creep was for real. We formulated a plan between us. The next time he came in she would let us know and we would take it from there. A few days later he came in with a big briefcase looking very important and sat at the counter. She came over and whispered to us, "That's him. Our time had come!"

I must point out that William and I were in our prime at that time. We were both big burly cowboy type guys. I stood six foot six inches tall and spent a few days each week in the gym and William was also over six foot tall and in good condition. We slowly ambled over to where he was sitting and approached him from both sides. I slid up next to him and put my arm on his shoulder and leaned down hard. He was startled and looked up at me.

I smiled and said, "Howdy, I hear you want to put my sister in the movies." A look of terror came over him as he began to tremble and shudder.

William on the other side said, "We just want to check everything out to protect our little sister."

By then he had broken out in a cold sweat and babbled incoherently about only wanting to help her get started and knowing a lot of people in Hollywood who could help her.

All the waitresses behind the counter watched and were in near hysterics as the scene unfolded. The more the guy tried to weasel his way out of the situation, the more pressure I applied to his shoulder. It was almost more than William and I could do to keep from breaking up for we could see this poor little creep was about to wet himself or have a stroke.

Finally we let up and told him that any interview he had with our Sister, we would come with her.

He quickly paid his bill and left, never to return to that coffee shop. It turned out that he was just some two for a nickel extra trying to impress and take advantage of a pretty young girl in Hollywood. After that William and I were kings and heroes with the waitresses and staff and had fouled another dastardly Hollywood plot!

THE LEGEND OF O.K. FREDDIE

The next story about a Hollywood is just a might off color. So if you are easily offended by such stories, this would be a good time to take a potty break or just skip to another story.

The story, or should I say legend of O.K. Freddie, has been one of those Hollywood stories that has floated around for many years, and I have heard several versions with just a few differences. The first time I heard the story was in the 1960s while at a party at actor Burt Lancaster's house. I will relate that version here.

As with so many Hollywood parties, most of the time is spent listening to stories about happenings on this or that film shoot, some very funny others just plain boring. As to be expected, Mr. Lancaster was the center of attraction telling some great tales of his adventures in the film industry. One story he told was about a well-known extra in Hollywood at that time called O.K. Freddie.

It seems that O.K. was well endowed, or should I say hung like a horse and much larger than the average man, and because of that gift became well known in the industry. It was said that for a few bucks O.K. would readily display his manhood and that got him a lot of work. He became well known, a legend in his own time, and he was called upon many times to play practical jokes on many of the elite crowd in Hollywood.

This story happened at the wrap party of a film in which Barbara Stanwyck was one of the stars. She was well known in the industry as a great lady and she loved a practical joke. Everybody at the party thought it would be great fun to play a joke on her.

It was all arranged and O.K. Freddie was called in. The prop man rigged one of the serving trays with a cut-out at one end. Freddie placed his member through the cut-out (that pretty much filled the tray), garnishes of various kinds were placed around it and a quick splash of barbecue sauce, made it look very tasty. Freddie, dressed as a waiter and with tray in hand, went directly to Miss Stanwyck and offered her a snack from his tray. Before anyone could stop her, she took the large fork from the tray and plunged it into Freddie's member thinking it was a prop. All hell broke loose as Freddie let out a blood curdling scream and fainted, scaring Miss Stanwyck half to death.

After that incident it is said that nobody saw poor old Freddie for quite a while and that when they did his voice had gone up a few octaves. Later Miss Stanwyck told everyone she thought it was a rubber prop and was going along with the gag because she thought it would get a laugh!

All things in Hollywood don't always go off as planned!

THE GOOD OLD DAYS

I remember back in the late 1940s just after the war ended, my Mother told me Dad was bringing cowboy star, Tex Ritter, to the ranch to look at one of our horses. That was great, Tex Ritter coming to our little ranch. WOW! I hopped on my trusty Schwinn bicycle and headed out to spread the word. I was like Paul Revere. I let everyone in and around our ranch know that Tex Ritter was coming! After making the fastest trip around the neighborhood in history, I rushed to my room to get properly dressed for his arrival.

Then the moment was at hand. My dad pulled through our ranch gate followed by a big new white pickup truck pulling a shiny new horse trailer. He had arrived! By that time there were six or eight kids all decked out in our finest cowboy duds, six-guns and spurs all shined up, we looked fine. Then his truck door opened and out stepped Tex wearing a big white Stetson hat and a big grin.

I remember he looked at us and asked my dad, "Who is this tough looking bunch of cowboys?"

Dad answered him, "That's the local gang."

I guess even in those days I was a bit of a smartass for I piped up saying, "We ain't no gang. We're good guys just like you."

As my dad showed him around the ranch and the horse he came to see, we kids were just one step behind him. Tex was one of our heroes, we saw all of his films and serials, and heck it's wasn't every day we got to meet one of our heroes!

My mother and a couple of the local ladies had prepared a nice lunch for everyone. I believe half of our neighborhood showed up to see a real movie star in person.

My dad was interested in guns and asked him if he had any of his show guns with him. Tex went to his rig and brought out a beautiful pair of fancy Colt pistols and holsters and a rope. He allowed all of us kids to hold and admire those treasures. He showed us some fancy gun spinning and a few tricks with his pistols and then did a few tricks with his rope. I was even roped by Tex Ritter; it doesn't get any better than that for a nine year old kid.

He loaded the horse he bought from my dad and signed photo's for all of us kids. I still have mine hanging on the wall in my office. It was a big event in our lives and everyone seemed to enjoy it very much. It's one of those things one never forgets because in those days we kids had real heroes to look up to and we watched them each Saturday at our local movie theatre. They taught us respect and a sense of honor. They taught us right from wrong and a deep love for our country, something lacking in today's so called heroes who kids watch and idolize. It was a better time in America, and I miss it.

I was fortunate that my dad was a wheeler-dealer and horse trader. I got to meet a few of my cowboy heroes because of his dealings. I remember Slim Pickens, Ben Johnson, Allen (Rocky) Lane and Andy Devine coming to our little ranch to deal with my dad. It was always exciting to see what happened next. Dad was a real character involved in all sorts of dealing and trading, if it was worth a buck he would buy or sell it, and because of those dealings some real outlaws came through our lives.

I remember one afternoon my dad and his brother pulled into the ranch with a pickup load of slot machines. They quickly emptied the tack room of saddles and gear and replaced them with the machines. I was told not to go near them and not to say a word to anyone about them being there. Well, being a kid and curious, as soon as they left I was in the room admiring the wonderful machines with all the colors and designs, it was too much for me to keep to myself. I think I showed them to every kid in the neighborhood.

About a week later my mother got a frantic phone call from my dad. He told her to have me take all the machines out to the pasture, break them up, and bury them as fast as I could. I, and one of my pals, loaded two machines at a time onto a wheelbarrow, took them to the pasture and dumped them in a hole. It took us about an hour to get the job done. We thought it would be great fun to have some target practice before we covered them. We shot the machine to pieces until we ran out of ammo and then covered the hole. That afternoon a few fellows pulled into the ranch with a search warrant and began going through everything. They found nothing and left.

I think about that little adventure quite often and wonder

what those machines would be worth today, and what the developers of that land must have thought when they uncovered these old relics.

BECOMING A HOLLYWOOD MAKE-UP ARTIST

My first day on the set as a make-up artist was one I will never forget and still laugh about to this day.

After serving my apprenticeship in the lab at MGM Studios, I had my first chance to actually go on set as a full-fledged make-up artist. My assignment that morning was to report to the set of the television series, "Man form Uncle," and help the make-up man. I was all full of myself and quite confident that I could handle most anything they might throw at me. I was going to prove myself and show them that the long months of training had paid off, and I could be an asset to the studio.

When I walked into that big sound stage that first day, I knew I had found my place in the world. It felt like I had come home, I had worked long and hard for that moment. I was greeted by the first assistant director, "Hello Mr. Fleming, your work area is all ready for you. Welcome to the set!"

Wow, I thought, *they know my name, even called me mister, and have an area all ready and waiting for me.* I was led to an area behind set where the dressing rooms and make-up tables were set up, it was all very professional. I was shown my table and told to get set up, have a cup of coffee and they would send me my first actor in a few minutes. I opened my shiny new make-up case for the first time on the set as a full-fledged make-up artist, and boy was I proud! After setting up my tools and making ready for my first victim, I went out on the set to introduce myself to the head make-up man and director. I was welcomed to the set and told they would send my first actor to me in a few minutes.

My first job would be to makeup a stuntman to double David McCallum, who was one of stars of the show. I thought, *This couldn't be too hard. Surely they cast someone who looked similar to Mr. McCallum.* When I got to my table everything around the table and dressing rooms was pitch black except for a key light which lit on my table. That was not unusual. They often turned off all of the lights on the stage when shooting so they would not get any light leaks or flairs while filming. I sat down in the make-up chair with my cup of coffee and waited for my first make-up job to arrive.

In a few minutes he made his appearance, and I almost had a heart attack. He was a big burly stuntman who looked nothing like the actor he would be doubling. My heart raced as I tried to figure out how to pull it off. I tried to keep calm and look professional as I had him take a seat in the make-up chair, all the while looking at his face and trying to figure out what to try first. I saw that his nose was not right so I began building it up using mortician's wax and doing some creative highlighting and shadowing around it and the eyes. His face was much wider than McCallum's so I tried desperately to make it look more narrow with shadowing. I looked at my work and knew I was in big trouble, for no matter what I tried, he still did not look right. I went into a mild panic but kept trying. It had to work, it was my first chance to prove myself, and I could not blow it or my career might be over. I applied false eyebrows and mustache to match our actor and stepped back to look at my handiwork. Oh my God. He looked like Quasimodo from the "Hunchback of Norte Dame."

Now I was in full panic mode. I didn't know what to do. I had screwed up big time, and thought my career was over. The poor stuntman looked at me and said he thought something was not quite right with the make-up and maybe we should change it a bit. That was all I needed to hear.

I broke out in a sweat, my hands trembled, I thought my heart was going to jump out of my chest . . . I wanted to run!

From the darkened area around me I began to hear faint snickers, then bursts of full-fledged hilarious laughter. I thought the stuntman was going to fall out the chair he laughed so hard. The stage lights came on and there was the entire crew watching me, the whole thing had been set up as a big joke and they began to applaud. They all had a good laugh on me that day and I guess I passed their test. After that, I was part of the crew.

I was really green in those early days and did not know that most of the time stuntmen are usually so far away from the camera, or has his back to the camera, so almost anyone near the same size and build can double the actor with very little make-up.

ADVENTURES IN MEXICO

While shooting a film in Mexico City called "The Hand" with my good friend Samantha Eggar, I had lots of free time to explore the city. My girlfriend was with me on that location so we spent most of our time looking for antiques.

One morning we headed to the Loginea Thieves' Market, one of Mexico's oldest and biggest street markets. It was a wonderful place for collectors or people just looking for something different to do while in Mexico. It had anything you could imagine from priceless antiques to bits and pieces of junk brought out of the hills by peons. We arrived at the market just before sunrise and began our search. It was a magical place with all the different cultures and treasures people were setting up, it was like watching a city come to life. My kind of place! We spent the first few hours buying little things and having a great time.

I came to one vendor's stand and noticed an antique Colt

revolver among his goods. Being an avid gun collector, I immediately asked permission to look at it. As I examined it I noticed a man watching me from across the aisle. I fumbled around a bit and then put the gun back on the table. I wanted to buy it but was a bit worried about being watched by a guy who looked like a Mexico City cop. I told my girlfriend to walk up a few aisles and wait for me, that I was going back to buy the revolver and might be arrested for having a gun in Mexico.

When I bought the gun, sure enough I was approached by this man. "Excuse me, but did you just buy a gun from that man?" he asked.

I thought, *Oh shit. I'm going to a Mexican jail.* I told him that I had indeed bought an antique revolver, and asked if there was any problem.

He smiled and stuck out his hand and said, "My name is Roberto Green. I am a gun collector also. What are you doing in Mexico?"

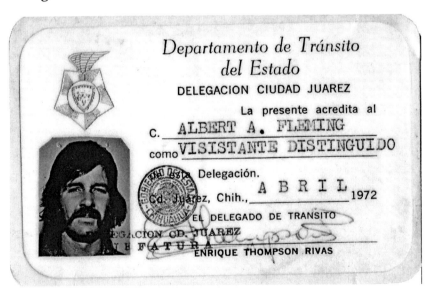

I told him we were filming a movie at Churubusco Studio and would be there for another three weeks. It turned out that he was the ballistics expert for the police department and army and loved movies. It was a very lucky meeting for Roberto opened doors for us that very few gringos get to see. He got me a permit to carry a gun while I was in Mexico and loaned me one of his. It was funny for when he gave me the permit and gun, he told I could shoot anyone I wanted except a policeman or politician. I assured him I did not want to shoot anyone but would feel more comfortable having some protection when I went into some of the off the track places looking for antiques.

When I returned to the studio, I told some of the American crew what had happened and that Roberto said if there was anything we wanted or needed just let him know. Jokingly, a couple said to tell him we need some smoke. Of course, they were only kidding. One evening while having dinner with him I jokingly asked if we would get in trouble if we were caught smoking weed.

He looked at me and said, "Why, do you want some marijuana?"

I didn't know what to say. I looked at my girlfriend and she shrugged her shoulders. "Well, I don't want to get in any trouble."

"I'll get you some." And that was all that was said.

The next afternoon there was a knock on our door. My girlfriend peeked through the peephole and whispered to me, "There's some thug looking guy at the door. What should I do?" I opened the door a bit and he handed me a large garbage bag.

"From Senor Green," he said, and he left.

When I opened the bag my heart almost stopped. There was nearly five pounds of top quality marijuana in the bag. I thought, *What do I do now?* The next day I gave most of it to our American crew members who couldn't believe that I had actually asked and received marijuana from a high ranking Mexican official.

The next time I saw Roberto, he asked one thing pertaining to the marijuana. He asked that no one try to take any of it back to the U.S. when we left. I assured him that nobody would take anything back with them. When we finished our last day shooting on the film I had about a pound of weed still up in our room. We were on the third floor at the upscale El Presidente Hotel right on the main avenue through Mexico City. My problem was what to do with the stuff before we left the next day. After pondering the subject for a while, I still had not come up with an answer. The next morning as we prepared to leave the hotel for our flight home, I stepped out onto the balcony and emptied the bag of marijuana into the air. It rained down on the sidewalk below where the hotel crew was filling the drinking water bottles for the rooms right out of the city water faucets (Ever wonder why you get the runs in Mexico even though you are drinking from so-called sterile water supplied to your rooms?).

Filming in Mexico was always an adventure if you just got away from the tourists area and did a little exploring on your own. I guess with the present world situation it might not be as safe as it used to be. When I lived there in the 1960s it was a beautiful country with kind warm people and great places to explore. I would wander into places that I was told were unsafe for Americans and that it was too dangerous to go there alone. I never had one problem even though I did go into some areas where I was a bit uneasy looking for antiques.

I will relate a story that could have had a very bad ending. I had a habit of going into downtown Guadalajara every morning to have breakfast with a few friends of mine. We ate at a small sidewalk cafe right across the street from the Hotel Fenix (at that time a nicer American type hotel). It was April 17, 1961, the day Cuba was invaded by American and Cuban freedom fighters (Bay of Pigs).

None of us knew anything about what had happened but

saw large crowds of people gathering in the streets carrying red flags and marching while chanting. At first I thought it was some kind of Mexican celebration or parade and paid not much attention to it. One of the waiters told us that it was an anti-American demonstration and that we might not be safe sitting outside. He suggested that we go inside and finish our meal. After breakfast we all decided it might be a good idea to go home to wait out the situation and see what happened.

I lived three miles from town and always walked to and from the café. That day wasn't going to be any different, besides I didn't have the cost of a cab ride. So I walked through the crowds of demonstrators and headed home. I did get some dirty looks and some name calling, but I still didn't speak Spanish that well so I don't know what was said. When I arrived back home (I, and two other Americans, rented the top floor of a very nice old hacienda in a nice area), I was met by the owner. My two pals who were very upset and told me that anti-American mobs were burning and looting American homes just a few blocks away. They were heading our way. The owner had called the police but did not expect help to arrive in time. There was not much we could do except to wait and hope that the police would get everything under control, and if you know anything about Mexican police you know that's wasn't likely to happen.

I made up my mind that if I was going down, I would go down fighting. I went upstairs and got the only weapon that I had a few rounds for, an 1877 Colt pump lightning rifle in 44-40 caliber. I had five rounds, which I loaded, and went out on the veranda and waited. We could see smoke and hear the noise of the rioters as they neared our street, then we saw them as they rounded the corner about six houses from ours. My heart was pounding so hard I thought I would most likely have a heart attack and die before the rioters could kill me. I cranked a round into the chamber of my rifle, lay down and started taking aim at the approaching mob, ready to take a few of them with me. Like in a movie, we then heard sirens and loudspeakers blaring, and the Mexican army and police came crashing into the mob. High pressure fire hoses quickly dispersed the crowd and sent them on their way.

So the last stand on Parque Juan Diego never happened, and I am here to tell you the story. It turned out that just two houses away from where we were, a high ranking Mexican Army General lived and that is the only reason the army showed up. This is a true story!

CORRIGANVILLE

I must mention Corriganville which played a big part of my early years in Hollywood.

When I first arrived in California and slowly got involved in the film industry, I was drawn to the old western movies and the stars I had watched growing up as a kid in Florida. I don't remember who it was but somewhere along the way Corriganville and the western stunt shows they put on each weekend was mentioned. That was all I needed, I headed there the next weekend. I paid my two dollar entrance fee and was ready for some western thrills. It was great fun. They put on some pretty good shows all day long, and as a young southern kid, I thought it was well worth my two bucks. I was thrilled to meet Crash Corrigan and have my picture taken with him. I told Crash that I was new to Hollywood and just started in the film industry.

He told me of the Crash Corrigan School of Dramatic Acting classes he ran at the ranch, and asked me if I was interested in becoming a student. I jumped at the chance to be able to work with one of the western stars I had grown up watching as a kid. But there was a catch, they charged to attend the school and I was living pretty close to the edge financially in those days. I explained that to him and he told

188

me they had a plan where I could work in the shows on the weekends to pay the tuition. So that is how I became a Corriganville actor and stuntman.

It turned out that the so called school of dramatic acting was nothing more than a scam to get free performers for the street shows every weekend. I must admit it was fun and I did learn a lot about stunt work and very little about real acting. Every weekend we would put on six street shows narrated by Crash. It was rough and tumble all the way. We did roof falls, horse falls, fist fights and all sorts of gun play. After each weekend we would head to the Goodwill store to replace our torn up costumes and get ready for the next weekend's shows. I loved it. Hell, I was playing cowboy to a packed audience each weekend and after a year of doing shows I was even given a salary of a whopping five dollars a weekend (big money at Corriganville) and top billing in the shows. I was on my way to stardom!

One thing that helped out was the fact that when a film company used the ranch for a location, we all got to work as extras. I spent three years working at the ranch and had some great times, met some real nice folks, and I did learn

a lot! At one point Crash hit hard times and knew I loved the old western guns and holsters. He offered to sell me his Bolin saddle and two gun holster with his two Colt pistols for three hundred and fifty dollars (a lot of money in those days). Hell, I could not put fifty dollars together much less three hundred and fifty, so I had to pass . . . To this day I regret not being able to buy that stuff.

One thing that did come from working at the ranch was I met a young lady there who became my first wife!

A CLASS ACT
MOSES COMES TO THE MOUNTAIN

My good friend, Michael Branson, and I were elected to be the Bushway's, or leaders, or Big Chiefs of the N.M.L.R.A. (National Muzzle Loading Rifle Association) western states rendezvous in 1980. It was an annual gathering of people from all over the world who shared an interest in the early history of the American fur trade. The rendezvous or camp was held in the Rocky Mountain area of the west as close to an original rendezvous site as possible. That year's site was in a wilderness area about twenty miles from the small town of La Veta, Colorado. The rules of the event were simple: all camps, tools and clothing must be from the 1840s period or reproductions of that era, no modern items of any kind were allowed in camp except cameras, and they had to be kept out of sight.

Columbia Pictures called me a few months before the event was to take place. They wanted to know if they could bring a few actors, and the Hollywood press, to rendezvous to help promote a new film they were about to release called "The Mountain Men." After talking it over with Branson, we agreed that it might be fun for the camp to see and meet some Hollywood people, as long as they did not interrupt the camp too much and would go along with the rules we set up.

I spent many hours the next two month in meetings and on the phone with the people at Columbia laying down the rules they would have to follow to be allowed into camp. The rules were: everyone was required to dress in period costumes, all cameras had to be disguised in some way that did not interfere with the look of the camp, and the main body of the press had to remain in a group. When everything was agreed to and all the necessary papers had been signed everything was a go except that they wanted to bring a security team with them to watch out for the stars. We turned this down flat and told them that we would supply them with security from our Dog Soldiers (camp police).

HESTON'S DOG SOLDIERS

The night before they were to arrive at camp, Branson and I held a meeting in La Vita to meet the stars and press. We told them what to expect when they entered the camp and went over the rules again. We met Charlton Heston, Frasier Heston (director of the film and son of Charlton Heston) and

Victoria Rasimo that evening for the first time. It was all set for them to arrive at ten o'clock the next morning.

We held a camp meeting and told everyone what to expect when the Hollywood folks arrived. We asked that the camp give them a good old mountain man welcome. The next morning as Hollywood arrived, Branson and I greeted the procession riding our horses bareback dressed in our finest buckskins. Branson promptly fell off his horse and landed in a heap alongside the road, so I led them into camp. It was a great sight. The entire camp turned out dressed in their finest beaded buckskins and brightly colored Indian clothing, lining both sides of the trail leading into camp. As Heston and the press entered, they were greeted with a salute of musket and cannon fire sending plumes of black powder smoke into the air and cheers from the crowd, it was quite a sight and the press loved it.

Mr. Heston made a speech to the crowd thanking them for allowing him and the press to visit the camp. He said Columbia had made arrangements for the film to be shown, for the first time, right there in our Rocky Mountain camp the next evening. After all the speeches had been made and the press had the pictures they needed, we gave them a tour of the camp. The stars participated in a lot of the events we had planned. At the end of a long day, Mr. Heston asked me if he could stay in camp that night to get away from all the reporters that followed him everywhere he went. I told him there was plenty of room in my teepee and I had an extra buffalo robe he was welcome to use. My offer was quickly accepted.

That evening my girlfriend and I listened to Mr. Heston, or Chuck as he liked to be called, tell stories of his adventures in Hollywood's early days. We got to know him and found him to be a really wonderful person with a deep love for the country and its history. He was a class act. The next day he spent visiting with folks in the camp, asking questions and taking pictures, and just being one of the guys.

The crew from Columbia Pictures tried to erect a large portable screen to show the film that evening. But as usual in the Rocky Mountains, the winds came up and blew it down. The screen was torn in half making it impossible to show the film as promised. It was quickly arranged to show it the next evening at a drive in theatre some thirty miles from our camp.

What a sight it must have been the next evening. It looked like the grapes of wrath as the procession of campers, pickup trucks and various odd vehicles all loaded with bearded buckskin clad men, and brightly dressed women and kids, descended on the local drive in theater to watch the film. As the screen flickered to life and the film began cheers and a few musket blasts came from the audience but as the movie began a dead silence fell over the crowd. When the film ended some dummy, who had too many pulls on the white lightning jug, shot a hole through the screen with a cannon. After that is was a mad scramble of vehicles trying to get out of there before the local police arrived. It looked like a Chinese fire drill, everyone got away clean except one poor sole who forgot to take his speaker off his window and jerked the speaker stand out of the ground and destroyed his window. All ended well for Columbia stepped up and paid for all the damages.

I am sure the rendezvous at La Veta, Colorado will stand out in memories of every one who was there. Hollywood had come to the mountains and got many a wild stories for the press to use. For me—heck, I had spent two days in the mountains with Moses. What could be better than that? A few weeks after I had returned home I received a very nice letter from Mr. Heston thanking me for making the event happen. He told me that he had never felt so safe anywhere in the world as he had with his Dog Soldier security team at the rendezvous!

FUNNY HAPPENING

This story has nothing to do with Hollywood but thought I would share it with you anyway for it is a bit funny.

In my teenage years, I was an active skin diver when the sport was just starting. I lived in a very small town on Florida's west side called Crystal River, it was one of God's little treasures with crystal clear rivers and lakes and unsoiled wilderness all around, it was truly paradise in those days.

I met a man named Tom McQuarie who ran a fishing boat rental on the river. He also became fascinated with skin diving and offered me a job helping him start a small diving business we called Aqua Pier. We had two tanks that we rented and a compressor that we could fill them with. Our business was slow but grew as divers learned about our beautiful river.

I don't remember whose idea it was, but we came up with a plan to bring more money into the business. It that part of Florida there were a few water attractions, Silver Springs and Rainbow Springs, that offered the public glass bottom boat rides over their springs and down their rivers. Well we thought our river and big spring were as good, if not better, than theirs so why don't we do the same things?

Tom got a small glass bottomed boat (held six people plus the driver/diver) and I started taking tourists on underwater tours of our river, the climax was over the large spring and caverns that supplied most of the water to the river. It was a beautiful place with a very deep canyon filled with huge boulders, sparkling white sand and many caves. Occasionally we saw a family of manatees (sea cows) swimming there that would delight the folks.

We realized we needed more, something to bring more excitement to our viewers, something the other springs did not offer . . . we would add an underwater show! That is what we did. When we arrived at the big spring near the end of the tour, I donned diving gear and went over the side of the boat and down into the spring. I did a few stunts and then disappeared into one of the caves. I waited in the cave a few minutes, all the while releasing air from my tank which created lots of bubbles, and then I reappeared waving at our guests. Pretty corny I know, but I was a teenaged kid.

I came up with an idea to perhaps add more excitement to the show. As I got ready to enter the cave I would fake running out of air, desperately grasping at my air valve and start to gasp for air, go limp and slowly start to sink towards the bottom. Then I came back to life, wave at the viewers, and resurface. That seemed to be a big hit with everyone so it became part of our show.

One day as I was going into my poor drowning diver act, the big climax of the show, and started my slow descent towards the bottom, I was suddenly grabbed from behind and quickly pulled to the surface. That scared the hell out of me. I didn't know what was going on. When I reached the surface, everyone in the boat was applauding and seemed relieved. When I regained my composure, I found a very pretty woman had me around the neck. She asked, "Are you okay?"

I tried to explain that it was all part of the show and that I was never in any real danger. At first she seemed angry then she broke into a big smile, pushed me away and climbed back into the boat. It was quite a show and everyone seemed to like it, except me. I felt like a fool! It turned out that my would-be-rescuer was none other than Ester Williams who was in Florida scouting locations for her upcoming movie, "Dangerous When Wet."

Another thing that happened while I was at Aqua Pier was that Jacque Cousteau, the great undersea explorer, came to Crystal River to film one of his so called true adventures. We were hired to help herd manatees (sea cows) into a small secluded spring right off the river where Cousteau planned to film. The crew arrived first, most all Frenchmen and divers working for Cousteau on this project. We found most of them to be arrogant and stuck up and not very friendly to us country boys.

It was a job and paid pretty good money for doing something we liked anyway, so we just ignored them and did our job. We asked many questions about why they wanted the manatees in a location where they were never found, but we got no answer. When Cousteau's son arrived on location, he took charge of everything and before they started shooting he fired us local boys.

The area where they were shooting was closed to everyone except their crews. There was always tight security around the area, and none of us locals knew what was going on. Months later when the show was aired on television, we could not believe what was presented as a true story. Someone had made up a story about how the manatees had lived in that spring for hundreds of years and would migrate there every year to have their calves. What a crock that was, we all knew there had never been a manatee in that spring, for the entrance from the river had been blocked by fallen trees and underwater growth for years and the water was too shallow. That just shows you that you can't believe everything you see on television, even if it is presented as a true documentary. After that experience I always questioned anything Cousteau did.

A WONDERFUL ADVENTURE

Thinking back over my life I find that it has been one wonderful adventure, one that I could only dream about as a child. When I think about all the things that had to come together just at the right time to make my journey possible, I am amazed and thankful. What are the chances that a country kid raised in the swamps and wilderness of Florida could end up in Hollywood in the film industry? It still seems impossible to me even today, I have been very lucky!

Think about it. How likely was it that Elvis Presley, one of the world's biggest stars and one of my idols, would come to a small remote town on the west coast of Florida to make a movie, that by chance would be staying at the resort where I was working and, by some luck of the draw, I would get to meet and work with him? It all seems like a Hollywood script even when I think about it . . . It was the one big event in my life that changed the future for me. It led me to Hollywood and a life I never dreamed of. Because of that encounter, I have traveled all over the world, seen things that most people will never see, met and worked with some of the most famous people in the world and had some wonderful adventures.

It has not all been fun and games. Working on a film is very hard work, long hours, pushing yourself beyond your limits, very little rest or time for yourself. Looking back, however, it has all been worth it. It gave me a life full of adventure and excitement that I would have never known if it had not been for that magic summer of 1961, when my life was given a direction and changed forever. I have been following that dream ever since!

AL FLEMING lives in a small mountain community in southern California. His life has been one big adventure from the swamps of southern Florida to the bright lights of Hollywood. He has worked in the Hollywood film industry for over fifty years meeting and becoming friends with some of its elite. He is a multi-talented artist and historian who spends most of his time off in his studio carving wood, sculpting or restoring antique firearms. His love of the old west has led him down many different paths in the film industry from technical advisor to costume designer to actor. His story is an interesting look behind the scenes of Hollywood and of some of its most famous or notorious characters . . . He has surely been Following That Dream!

CPSIA information can be obtained
at www.ICGtesting.com
Printed in the USA
FSOW02n0432270716
23034FS